Wonder-Under®
Handmade Gifts

Oxmoor
House®

Wonder-Under® Handmade Gifts
from the *Fun with Fabric* series

©1998 by Oxmoor House, Inc.
Book Division of Southern Progress Corporation
P.O. Box 2463, Birmingham, Alabama 35201

Published by Oxmoor House, Inc., and
Leisure Arts, Inc.

Library of Congress Catalog Number: 98-65466
Hardcover ISBN: 0-8487-1684-1
Softcover ISBN: 0-8487-1685-X
Manufactured in the United States of America
First Printing 1998

Editor-in-Chief: Nancy Fitzpatrick Wyatt
Senior Crafts Editor: Susan Ramey Cleveland
Senior Editor, Editorial Services: Olivia Kindig Wells
Art Director: James Boone

Wonder-Under® Handmade Gifts

Editors: Catherine Corbett Fowler,
   Cecile Y. Nierodzinski
Copy Editor: Anne S. Dickson
Editorial Assistant: Heather Averett
Associate Art Director: Cynthia R. Cooper
Designer: Carol Damsky
Illustrator: Kelly Davis
Senior Photographer: John O'Hagan
Photo Stylist: Linda Baltzell Wright
Senior Production Designer: Larry Hunter
Publishing Systems Administrator: Rick Tucker
Director, Production and Distribution: Phillip Lee
Associate Production Manager: Theresa L. Beste
Production Assistant: Faye Porter Bonner

We're Here for You!
We at Oxmoor House are dedicated to serving you
with reliable information that expands your imagina-
tion and enriches your life. We welcome your com-
ments and suggestions. Please write us at:

Oxmoor House, Inc.
Editor, *Wonder-Under® Handmade Gifts*
2100 Lakeshore Drive
Birmingham, AL 35209

To order additional publications, call 1-205-877-6560.

Pellon and Wonder-Under are registered trademarks of
Freudenberg Nonwovens. To locate a Pellon® Wonder-
Under® retailer in your area, call 1-800-223-5275.

CONTENTS

● ■ ♥ ★ ● ■ ♥ ★ ●

❤ Shower Gifts

★ Christmas Gifts

Acknowledgments 160

Introduction

Finding the perfect gift is always a challenge. But giving a handmade gift doesn't have to be. Pellon® Wonder-Under®, the quick way to appliqué, is the solution to your gift-crafting needs. The leading brand of paper-backed fusible web, Wonder-Under® is quick and easy to use, and it allows your creativity to show through with no sewing required. In *Wonder-Under® Handmade Gifts*, we'll show you dozens of ways to make gifts for family, friends, brides-to-be, and mothers-to-be, as well as yourself.

● Celebrate all the birthdays in your family—even your pet's special day! In **Birthday Gifts,** our ideas represent a wide range of passions, from gardening to home decor.

■ Welcome your new neighbors to the block with a gift that shows off your crafting talent. **Housewarming Gifts** inspires new ways to package and present your gift.

♥ Shower a mother-to-be or bride-to-be with keepsakes from the **Shower Gifts** chapter. Sachets and baby rompers are just a sampling of possibilities.

★ Wrap up something handmade for the holidays. In **Christmas Gifts,** we give simple patterns that you can use on a variety of items. A mitten and hat set are just the beginning.

General Instructions

Pellon® Wonder-Under® is a paper-backed fusible web, a heat-activated adhesive with a temporary paper lining. A hot iron melts the glue, fusing fabrics together. The web holds fabrics in place and prevents raveling. With Wonder-Under®, you don't have to sew a stitch!

Choosing the Correct Weight

Wonder-Under—Regular Weight and Heavy Duty—is available at fabric and crafts stores, off the bolt or in several prepackaged widths and lengths. It also comes in a ¾"-wide precut tape, 10 yards long, that is ideal for fusing hems and ribbons.

• Test different weights to find the Wonder-Under that best suits your project. Generally, you can use regular-weight web for light-weight to medium-weight fabrics. For heavyweight fabrics, a heavy-duty web is best. (Heavy Duty Wonder-Under has more glue and, therefore, more "stick.")

• For an appliquéd garment, heavy-duty web may add too much stiffness. Use regular-weight web and finish the edges of the appliqué as necessary to ensure a washable garment. (See washable fabric paint under Embellishment Techniques on page 8.)

• For projects in this book, Regular Weight Wonder-Under is usually recommended, unless Heavy Duty is specified.

• The Wonder-Under package label gives tips on its application and washability.

• Test Wonder-Under on scraps of fabric before you start your actual project. Let the sample cool and then check to see that the fabric pieces have bonded and that the fused layers won't separate.

Perfect Patterns

Wonder-Under is translucent, so you can place the web (paper side up) directly onto a pattern for tracing.

• If a pattern isn't the size you want, enlarge or reduce it using a photocopier.

• If a pattern has an asymmetrical or one-way design, the finished appliqué will be a mirror image of the pattern. So if a pattern points left, the appliqué will point right. In this book, patterns are reversed as necessary.

Fusing Basics

1. If the project you are making has an appliqué pattern, trace the pattern onto the paper (smooth) side of the Wonder-Under. Leaving a margin, cut around the shape.

2. For all Wonder-Under projects, place the web side of the Wonder-Under on the wrong side of the fabric. Press for 5 seconds with a hot, dry iron. Let the fabric cool. (If some of the Wonder-Under sticks to your iron, remove it with a hot-iron cleaner, available in most notion departments of fabric and crafts stores.) For appliqués, cut out the shape along the pattern lines.

3. Remove the paper backing from the Wonder-Under.

4. Position the fabric, web side down, on your project. (Fusible items can be held temporarily in place by "touch basting." Touch the item to be fused with the tip of the iron only. If the item is not in the desired position, it can be lifted and repositioned.)

5. To fuse, cover the fabric with a damp pressing cloth, unless otherwise specified. Using an iron heated to the wool setting, press firmly for 10 seconds. (Heavy fabrics may require more time.) Repeat, lifting and pressing until all the fabric is fused.

6. Remove the pressing cloth and iron the fabric to eliminate excess moisture.

Embellishment Techniques

Details, or embellishments, add a finishing touch to your project. They can also be functional. Pellon® Wonder-Under® holds appliqués securely in place, but with repeated use, some fraying may occur. To prevent this, consider adding one of the following finishes to fabric appliqués.

Washable fabric paint makes a good no-sew finish. Available at craft stores, these paints come in squeeze tubes that allow you to outline an appliqué with a thin line of paint. Place cardboard under the appliqué to prevent seepage, and follow the manufacturer's directions for drying time; some paints require several days to set. Most manufacturers recommend washing the finished project in warm water.

If you prefer a machine-stitched finish, a **decorative zigzag** also adds security to edges. Closely spaced zigzag stitches—or satin stitching—give shapes strong definition and completely encase raw edges. Even multiple layers of fabric fused with Heavy Duty Wonder-Under can be satin-stitched.

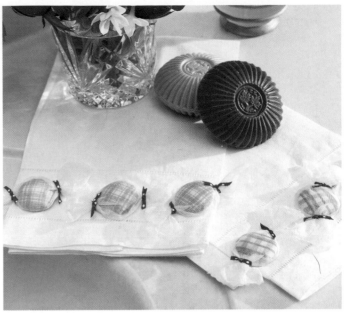

Fine-tipped fabric markers make it easy to add detail. You can use fine-tip markers to draw "quilting lines" around the edges of an appliqué. This technique is sometimes called pen stitching.

Buttons and beads add dimension and sparkle. Sewn or glued in place, they can represent ornaments, candy, and other objects.

You can also glue **twine, rickrack, braid, lace, or other trims** to your project to give extra dimension or color.

Birthday Gifts

There's no better way to explore the options of Wonder-Under® than with all the birthdays that you'll be celebrating throughout the year. Put together a bunch of sweet-smelling drawer liners or appliqué a pair of garden gloves that will brighten someone's day.

Ribbon Key Rings

Materials
(for 1 key ring)

Pellon® Wonder-Under® scraps

Grosgrain ribbon: 7" (1"-wide), 3" (⅜"-wide) in same color

Liquid ravel preventer

Fabric scraps for appliqués

Fabric glue

Seed beads: 7 yellow for leaf key ring; 12 multicolored for flower key ring; 6 white, 2 black, and 1 orange for snowman key ring; 7 black for watermelon key ring; and 1 pearl for tulip key ring

Spring-type clothespin

1½"-diameter metal key ring

Looking for an inexpensive gift idea? Make a set of seasonal key rings. Or for year-round use, make a colorful floral key ring.

Designed by Carol Tipton

Instructions

1. Cut 1 (1") square from Wonder-Under. Press square to 1 cut end of 7" ribbon. Remove paper backing. With sides aligned, fold end of ribbon under along inner edge of Wonder-Under square. Fuse in place.

2. Cut notch in opposite raw end of ribbon. Coat edges of ribbon with liquid ravel preventer. Let dry.

3. Press Wonder-Under onto wrong side of fabric scraps. Trace desired patterns on Wonder-Under side of fabric scraps. Cut out shapes along pattern lines. Remove paper backing. Referring to photo, fuse shapes onto ribbon.

4. Referring to photo, glue seed beads in place on ribbon. Let dry.

5. Fold 3" ribbon in half, matching ends. Glue ends together, forming loop. Secure with clothespin until glue dries. Glue cut ends of ribbon loop to back of folded end of ribbon. Use clothespin to hold ribbon loop in place until glue dries.

6. Thread key ring through ribbon loop.

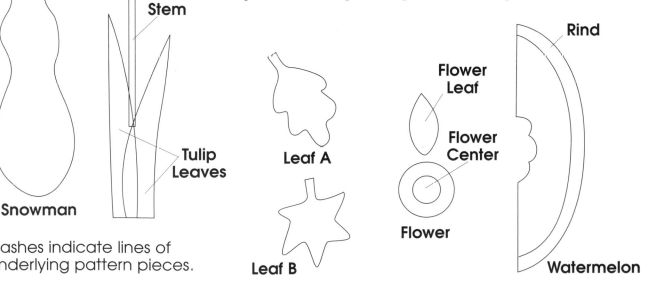

Hat

Tulip

Stem

Snowman

Tulip Leaves

Leaf A

Leaf B

Flower Leaf

Flower Center

Flower

Rind

Watermelon

Dashes indicate lines of underlying pattern pieces.

Proud Grandparent Sweatshirt

This sweatshirt provides a clever way for grandparents to show off their grandkids. For a truly personal touch, use scraps from the grandkids' worn-out clothes to make the appliquéd outfits.

Designed by Betsy Cooper Scott

Materials

Purchased plain sweatshirt
Fabric scraps for appliqués
Tracing paper
Black Sulky® Iron-on Transfer Pen
Pellon® Wonder-Under® scraps
Cardboard covered with waxed paper
Dimensional fabric paints in squeeze bottles: red, eye color for each grandchild, hair color for each grandchild, green, yellow
Disappearing-ink fabric marker

Instructions

1. Wash, dry, and iron sweatshirt and fabrics. Do not use fabric softener in washer or dryer.

2. Using pencil and patterns on page 16, trace desired body outlines on tracing paper. Trace over pencil lines (except eyes and mouths) using Sulky pen. Referring to photo and pen manufacturer's instructions, iron body outlines on front of sweatshirt.

3. Trace desired clothing pieces onto paper side of Wonder-Under. Leaving approximate ½" margin, cut around Wonder-Under shapes. Press shapes onto wrong side of fabric scraps. Cut out clothes along pattern lines. Remove paper backing. Referring to photo, position clothes over body outlines. Fuse clothes in place.

4. Place cardboard covered with waxed paper inside sweatshirt. Paint mouths using red fabric paint. Let dry. Paint eyes using desired fabric paint. Let dry. Paint hair using desired fabric paint. Let dry. Referring to photo, paint grass with green fabric paint and paint flowers with yellow fabric paint. Let dry. Referring to photo and using disappearing-ink fabric marker, write "All my Grandkids" under children. Paint over letters with green fabric paint. Let dry.

5. To launder, refer to paint manufacturer's instructions.

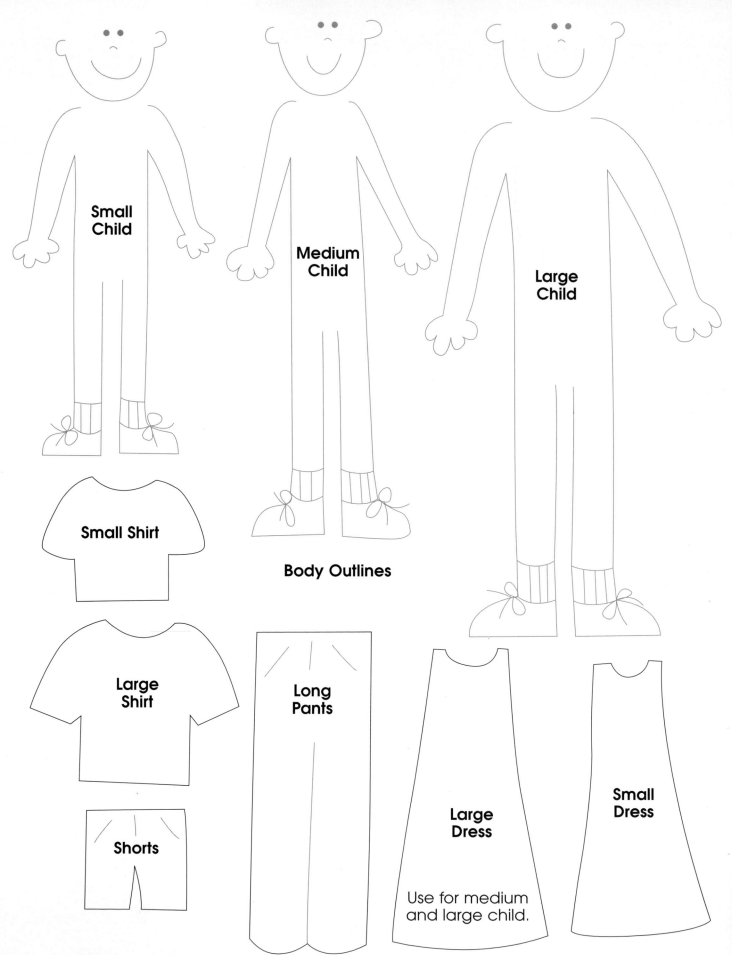

Small
Child

Medium
Child

Large
Child

Small Shirt

Body Outlines

Large
Shirt

Long
Pants

Large
Dress

Small
Dress

Shorts

Use for medium
and large child.

Computer Desk Set

Surprise the computer enthusiast in your life with this matching monitor frame and mouse pad. The frame has a cork base so notes can be tacked to it.

Designed by Alisa Jane Hyde

Materials

For Both:

Fabric for frame, pad, and
appliqués: 1 yard navy
blue; ¼ yard each gray,
yellow, red, black
Pellon® Heavy Duty
Wonder-Under®

For Computer Frame:

Black photo mat board (See
Step 1 for amount.)
Craft knife
¼"-thick cork board* (See
Step 2 for amount.)
Hot-glue gun and glue sticks
4 (3"-long) Velcro strips with
adhesive backs
Map pins or pushpins
(optional)

For Mouse Pad:

Plain, soft mouse pad without plastic top**
1 yard ⅝"-wide golden yellow grosgrain ribbon
Liquid ravel preventer

* Available at home-
improvement centers
** Available at office-supply
stores

Instructions for Computer Frame

Note: To prolong the wear
of the frame and mouse pad,
spray finished projects with
water-repellent fabric protector spray.

1. Measure height and
width of computer screen.
(Do not include frame of
monitor in measurements.)
Using pencil, draw these
dimensions on mat board.
Add 2" to sides and bottom
of screen measurement and
3½" to top of screen mea-
surement. Mark this area on
mat board (see Diagram A).
Using craft knife, cut out
screen area from mat board
to create frame opening; cut
out frame along outer lines.

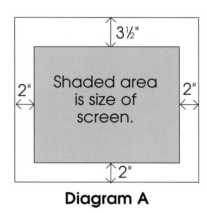

Diagram A

2. Repeat Step 1 to cut out
matching cork board frame.

3. To make frame base, with
edges aligned, hot-glue cork
frame to mat board frame.
(Cork will be front of frame
base and mat board will be
back of frame base.) Press
Wonder-Under onto wrong
side of navy fabric. Position
frame base on wrong side of
navy blue fabric. Using frame
base as guide and referring
to Diagram B, cut out fabric
"frame" that extends
approximately 2" beyond
each edge of frame base.

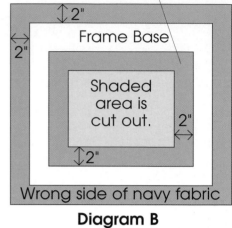

Diagram B

4. Referring to Diagram C,
trim notches from inside
edges of fabric frame as
shown. Remove paper back-
ing. Center fabric frame on
cork side of frame base.
Turn frame over. Wrap cut
edges of fabric to back of
frame base (mat board side)
and fuse. *(Note:* You may
need to gather fabric at outside corners of frame and
use hot-glue gun to secure
fabric.)

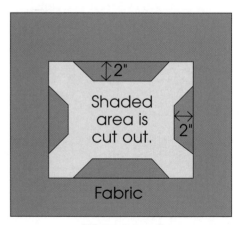

Diagram C

5. Trace 2 houses on mat
board. Cut out. Press
Wonder-Under onto wrong

side of gray, yellow, red, and black fabrics. Trace 2 large roofs, 3 medium roofs, and 3 small roofs on Wonder-Under side of gray fabric. Cut out roofs along pattern lines. Remove paper backing. Draw 2 (2¼" x 2⅞") rectangles on Wonder-Under side of yellow fabric. Draw 2 (1¾" x 2") rectangles, 3 (1½" x 2¾") rectangles, and 1 (1¼" x 1¾") rectangle on Wonder-Under side of red fabric. Draw 19 (½") squares and 2 (⅜") squares on Wonder-Under side of black fabric. Cut out shapes along lines. Remove paper backing.

6. With edges aligned, fuse 1 large gray fabric roof in place on each mat board house. With edges aligned, fuse 1 yellow fabric rectangle in place on each mat board house. Referring to photo, fuse 4 black fabric windows in place on each house. Set houses aside.

7. Referring to photo, fuse red fabric rectangles randomly on front of covered frame. Fuse gray fabric roofs in place on top of red rectangles. Fuse black fabric windows in place on houses. Referring to photo, hot-glue yellow houses in place on frame. *(Note:* Roofs of yellow houses extend above top edge of frame.)

8. To attach decorative frame to computer monitor, stick ½ of each Velcro strip to inside edge of computer monitor frame. With wrong sides up, stick remaining Velcro strips to inside edge of frame. Press frame to computer monitor, matching halves of Velcro strips.

9. Use map pins or pushpins to stick notes into decorative frame, if desired.

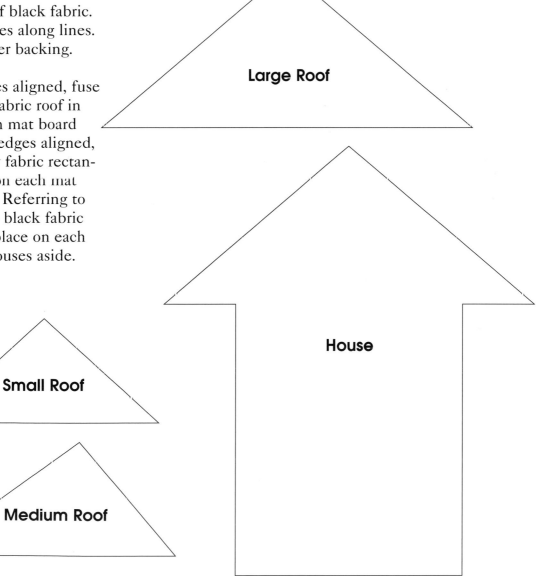

Large Roof

House

Small Roof

Medium Roof

Instructions for Mouse Pad

1. Press Wonder-Under onto wrong side of navy blue, gray, red, and black fabrics. Using mouse pad as pattern, trace mouse pad outline on Wonder-Under side of navy fabric. Cut out fabric mouse pad. Remove paper backing. Fuse navy fabric shape onto mouse pad.

2. Trace 1 large roof and 2 medium roofs onto Wonder-Under side of gray fabric. Draw 1 (2" x 4¼") rectangle, 1 (1½ x 3½") rectangle, and 1 (1¼" x 5") rectangle on Wonder-Under side of red fabric. Draw 6 (½") squares and 4 (¼") squares on Wonder-Under side of black fabric. Cut out shapes along drawn lines. Remove paper backing. Referring to photo, position houses on covered mouse pad. Fuse in place.

3. Cut 2 (8") lengths of ribbon and 2 (9") lengths of ribbon. Coat ends with liquid ravel preventer. Let dry. Cut 2 (⅝" x 8") strips and 2 (⅝" x 9") strips of Wonder-Under. Press 1 Wonder-Under strip to 1 side of corresponding ribbon. Remove paper backing. Referring to photo, fuse ribbons to covered mouse pad along edges.

Sun-brella

This sunny appliqué chases away rainy day blues. While the sun is an ideal motif for a child's umbrella, you can also make an adult version by substituting polka dots or a monogram.

Designed by Phyllis Dunstan

Materials

Purchased umbrella
Straight pins
Fabric marking pencil
Pellon® Heavy Duty
  Wonder-Under®
Fabric for appliqués: 7" x 12"
  piece yellow cotton, scrap
  black cotton
Dimensional fabric paints in
  squeeze bottles: black,
  blue glitter, red
Needle and thread to match
  umbrella (optional)

Instructions

Note: To waterproof umbrella, spray finished umbrella with a water-resistant protector.

1. Trace 1 face, 2 large sunbeams, and 3 small sunbeams on paper. Cut out shapes. Open umbrella. Referring to photo, position shapes on umbrella; pin. Trace around shapes with fabric marking pencil. Unpin shapes.

2. Trace 1 face, 2 large sunbeams, 3 small sunbeams, and 1 set of eyes onto paper side of Wonder-Under. Leaving approximate ½" margin, cut around shapes. Press face and sunbeam shapes onto wrong side of yellow fabric. Press eye shapes onto wrong side of black fabric. Cut out shapes along pattern lines. Remove paper backing from eyes only.

3. Referring to pattern for position, fuse eyes to face shape. Remove paper backing from remaining shapes.

4. To make fusing easier, if desired, snip tacking threads that hold umbrella fabric to spokes in marked section. Set iron on nylon setting. Using marked lines as guide, fuse shapes in place on umbrella.

5. Using black fabric paint and referring to pattern and photo, draw facial details. Let dry. Referring to photo, outline shapes with blue glitter fabric paint. Let dry. Use red fabric paint to add additional details to shapes. Let dry.

6. If you snipped tacking threads at spokes, use needle and doubled thread to retack umbrella fabric to spokes.

Other Ideas

Fuse decorative ribbon or trim onto an umbrella. Using ¾"-wide Pellon® Wonder-Under® tape on narrow trims makes it easier to decorate edges.

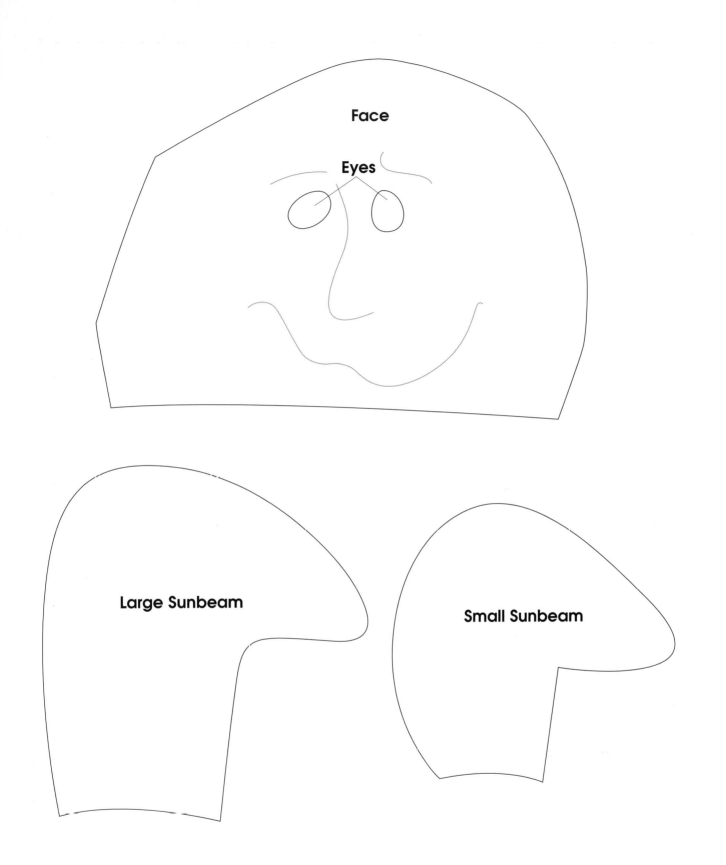

Face

Eyes

Large Sunbeam

Small Sunbeam

Gray lines are painted lines.

Bedecked Bulletin
Boards

Use novelty fabrics and Pellon® Wonder-Under® to customize a plain bulletin board. Because the fusible web won't bubble up the way glue can, your fabric will be smooth and neat.

Designed by Betsy Cooper Scott

Materials

For both:
18" x 24" cork bulletin board*
Pellon® Heavy Duty
    Wonder-Under®
Hot-glue gun and glue sticks

For Fabric-Covered Board:
½ yard fabric
5 yards ¼"-diameter sisal rope

For Ribbon-Trimmed Board:
White primer
Paintbrush
White enamel paint
Fabric for appliqués: ¼ yard
    each pink solid, pink-and-white stripe
Posterboard

* Be sure to purchase good-quality bulletin boards. Inexpensive ones tend to warp.

Instructions for Ribbon-Trimmed Board

1. Paint bulletin board with primer. Let dry. Paint bulletin board with enamel paint. Let dry.

2. Press Wonder-Under onto wrong sides of fabrics. Remove paper backing. Fuse fabrics to posterboard.

3. Working from fabric side of posterboard, on solid pink fabric, trace 1 entire bow, 1 entire bow reversed, and 3 Ribbon As. On pink-and-white stripe fabric, trace 2 Ribbon As, 1 outer bow, 1 outer bow reversed, 1 knot, and 2 Ribbon Bs. If desired, using 3" square as guide, draw "balloon" type letters for name or initials. Cut out shapes along pattern lines.

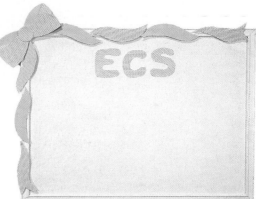

4. Hot-glue 1 pink-and-white stripe outer bow in place on corresponding entire bow shape. Repeat for other side. Referring to photo, hot-glue ribbon pieces to upper left corner of bulletin board, making sure to glue pieces to wooden frame. Hot-glue bow shapes and knot. If desired, hot-glue name or initials across top of cork area of bulletin board.

Instructions for Fabric-Covered Board

1. Cut fabric same size as cork area of bulletin board. Cut Wonder-Under piece to fit. Press Wonder-Under piece onto wrong side of fabric piece. Remove paper backing. Fuse fabric to cork area of bulletin board.

2. Referring to photo, cut sisal rope into 4 lengths to cover inside edge of frame. Hot-glue rope in place. Cut remaining sisal rope into 4 lengths to cover outside edge of frame. Hot-glue rope in place.

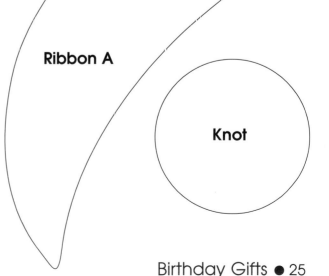

Ribbon B

Inner Bow

Outer Bow

Ribbon A

Knot

Funky Fabric Flowerpot

Materials

Clay pot
Fine-grit sandpaper
Sponge
1"-wide sponge brush
Water-based varnish
Pellon® Heavy Duty
   Wonder-Under® scraps
Fabric scraps for appliqués
Dimensional fabric paints in
   squeeze bottles in colors
   to coordinate with fabrics

Charm your best friend with a flowerpot embellished with fabric flowers in her favorite colors or in colors that coordinate with her home's decor.

Designed by Nancy Worrell

Instructions

1. Using fine-grit sandpaper, lightly sand clay pot to remove any flaws in clay. Wipe pot clean with slightly damp sponge. Let dry. Using sponge brush, apply coat of varnish to all surfaces of pot. Let dry.

2. Trace desired number of flowers, flower centers, and leaves on paper side of Wonder-Under. Leaving approximate ½" margin, cut around shapes. Press shapes onto wrong side of fabric scraps. Cut out shapes along pattern lines.

3. Remove paper backing from flower centers. Fuse flower centers onto flowers. Remove paper backing from remaining shapes. Referring to photo, fuse leaves to flowerpot. Fuse flowers to flowerpot. (You may need to fuse longer than usual to get a strong bond.)

4. Referring to photo and using dimensional fabric paints, outline shapes and add details as desired. Let dry.

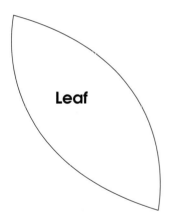

Leaf

Flower Center

Flower

All-the-Buzz Garden Gloves

Materials

Pellon® Heavy Duty
  Wonder-Under® scraps
Fabric scraps for appliqués:
  black, white
1 pair garden gloves
Dimensional fabric paints in
  squeeze bottles: black,
  yellow, silver glitter

Your gardening friends will love these busy bee gloves. The bee-coming appliqué adds a special touch to this practical gift.

Designed by Phyllis Dunstan

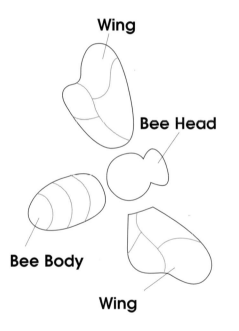

Wing

Bee Head

Bee Body

Wing

Gray lines are painted lines.

Instructions

1. Trace 2 bee heads, 2 bee bodies, and 2 sets of wings onto paper side of Wonder-Under. Leaving approximate ½" margin, cut out Wonder-Under shapes. Referring to photo for colors, press shapes onto wrong side of fabrics. Cut out shapes along pattern lines. Remove paper backing. Referring to photo for placement, fuse 1 set of bee shapes onto back of each glove.

2. Referring to pattern, use yellow fabric paint to paint 3 stripes on each bee body.

Let dry. Use black fabric paint to outline bee heads and bee bodies and to draw legs and antennae. Let dry. Referring to pattern, use silver glitter fabric paint to paint shapes inside wings. Outline wings and make eyes at top of each head, using silver glitter paint. Let dry.

Other Ideas

Use this appliqué on a gift card (see page 144) and box to give along with the gloves.

Sweet-Scented Drawer Liners

Materials
(for 1 container and 1 drawer liner)

Fabric: 7¾" x 13¾" piece to cover container, 13½" x 21½" piece for drawer liner

¾"-wide Pellon® Wonder-Under® fusible tape

Pellon® Wonder-Under®

Clean, empty oatmeal container

Ribbon: 13" (1½"-wide) for container, 2 yards 1"-wide for edging drawer liner, 18" (⅜"-wide) for tying drawer liner

Liquid ravel preventer

Fabric glue

1 tsp. perfume or cologne

Instructions

1. Machine-wash fabrics and ribbons, adding perfume to rinse cycle. Do not use fabric softener. Hang-dry.

2. To cover container, press fusible tape to wrong side of 1 short edge of 7¾" x 13¾" fabric piece. Remove paper backing. Fold edge of fabric to wrong side along inner edge of tape. Fuse in place. Repeat to hem 1 long edge.

3. Cut 7" x 13" piece of Wonder-Under. Press onto wrong side of hemmed fabric piece. Remove paper backing. Align long hemmed edge of fabric with bottom of oatmeal container, and fuse, making sure hemmed short edge covers raw short edge.

Bundle several perfumed drawer liners and wrap in a matching container for a feminine luxury any woman would love. Measure drawers to be lined and cut fabrics to fit.

Designed by Susan G. Peele

4. Coat end of 13" ribbon with liquid ravel preventer. Let dry. Cut 1 (1½" x 13") strip of Wonder-Under. Press Wonder-Under strip onto 1 side of 13" ribbon. Remove paper backing. Fuse ribbon around top of covered container, overlapping ends.

5. To make drawer liner, press fusible tape to wrong side of both short edges of 13½" x 21½" fabric piece. Remove paper backing. Fold short edges of fabric to wrong side along inner edges of tape. Fuse in place. Repeat to hem long edges.

6. Cut 1 (1" x 72") strip of Wonder-Under. (Strip may be pieced.) Press Wonder-Under strip onto 1 side of 72"-long ribbon. Remove paper backing. Fuse ribbon length to edges of right side of hemmed fabric piece, mitering corners. Use drop of fabric glue to hold each mitered ribbon corner in place. Let dry.

7. Roll drawer liner, beginning at 1 short end. Tie with 18" ribbon. Place liner in container.

8. If drawer liner begins to lose its fragrance, mist with perfume or wash as in Step 1.

Floppy Flower Hat

Materials

Hot-glue gun and glue sticks
Denim floppy hat
Pellon® Heavy Duty
    Wonder-Under® scraps
Fabric scraps for appliqués:
    yellow, brown felt
Dimensional fabric paint in
    squeeze bottles: yellow,
    brown
Wooden buttons: 7 (½"-
    diameter), 1 (⅝"-diameter)

A sunflower motif adds a touch of whimsy to a casual summer hat. The brim is hot-glued in place, so no sewing is required.

Designed by Barbara McNorton Neel

Instructions

1. Hot-glue front brim of hat to body of hat.

2. Press Wonder-Under onto wrong side of yellow fabric and onto 1 side of brown felt. Trace sunflower pattern onto Wonder-Under side of yellow fabric. Trace flower center pattern onto Wonder-Under side of brown felt. Cut out shapes along pattern lines. Remove paper backing.

3. Referring to photo, position sunflower on turned-up section of hat brim. (Top petals should extend onto body of hat.) Fuse sunflower in place. Fuse flower center onto sunflower.

4. Outline sunflower with yellow fabric paint. Let dry. Outline flower center with brown fabric paint. If desired, add detail lines to sunflower using brown fabric paint. Let dry.

5. Hot-glue small wooden buttons around edge of flower center, overlapping buttons as desired. Hot-glue large wooden button to center of flower.

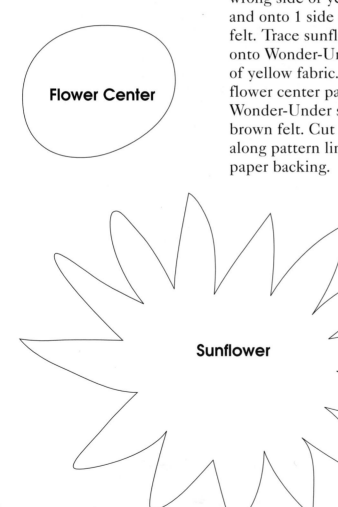

Flower Center

Sunflower

Picture Perfect Puppy Frame

Any devoted dog owner would love to display a photo of his loyal four-legged friend in this picture frame.

Designed by Alisa Jane Hyde

Materials

5" x 7" precut picture mat
Red bandanna
Pellon® Heavy Duty
    Wonder-Under®
Hot-glue gun and glue sticks
5" x 7" acrylic picture frame
2-oz. package white model-
    ing compound
Dog bone-shaped cookie
    cutter (optional)

Instructions

1. Position mat on wrong side of bandanna. Using mat as guide and referring to Diagram A, cut bandanna piece that extends approximately 1" beyond each edge of mat.

2. Cut Wonder-Under piece to fit bandanna piece. Press Wonder-Under onto wrong side of bandanna fabric. Referring to Diagram B, trim notches from inside edges of bandanna fabric as shown. Remove paper backing. Center and fuse bandanna fabric to front of mat. Turn mat over. Wrap cut edges of bandanna to back of mat and fuse. *(Note:* You may need to gather fabric at outside corners of mat and use hot-glue gun to secure fabric.)

3. With edges aligned, hot-glue covered mat to front of acrylic frame.

4. Roll out modeling compound to approximately ¼" thickness. Using pattern below or dog bone-shaped cookie cutter, cut out 3 dog bones. Following manufacturer's instructions, bake dog bones. Referring to photo for placement, hot-glue dog bones to front of frame.

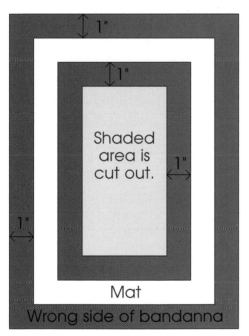

Diagram A

Diagram B

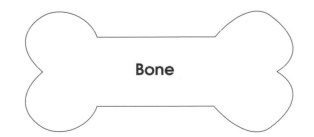

Bone

Tail-Wagging Treat Container

Materials

6½"-wide clay pot
6½"-wide clay saucer
Fine-grit sandpaper
Sponge
3 (1"-wide) sponge brushes
Water-based satin varnish
Acrylic craft paints: black, white
1 (1¾"-diameter) wooden ball
1 (¼"-wide) paintbrush (optional)
¼ yard white fabric (optional)
Pellon® Heavy Duty Wonder-Under®
Red bandanna
Heavy-duty epoxy glue
Doggie treats

Don't forget your best buddy's birthday! Reward his faithfulness with this clay pot container filled with doggie treats.

Designed by Alisa Jane Hyde

· ·

Instructions

1. Using fine-grit sandpaper, lightly sand clay pot and saucer to remove any flaws in clay. Wipe clean with slightly damp sponge. Let dry. Using sponge brush, apply coat of varnish to all surfaces of pot and saucer. Let dry.

2. Using sponge brush, apply 2 to 3 coats of black paint to all surfaces of pot and saucer, letting paint dry between coats. Let dry thoroughly. Using sponge brush, apply 2 coats of white paint to wooden ball, letting paint dry between coats. Let dry thoroughly.

3. To paint bones and paw prints on pot and saucer, referring to photo and using pencil, trace dog bone pattern randomly on sides of pot. Turn saucer upside down. Trace paw print pattern randomly on sides of saucer. Using ¼"-wide paintbrush and white paint, fill in traced bones and paw prints. Let dry. Paint light coat of varnish over entire pot and saucer. Let dry.

4. To fuse designs on pot and saucer, press Wonder-Under onto wrong side of white fabric. Trace approximately 8 dog bone shapes and 5 paw print shapes on Wonder-Under side of white fabric. Cut out shapes along pattern lines. Remove paper backing. Fuse dog bones randomly on sides of pot. Turn saucer upside down. Fuse paw prints randomly on sides of saucer.

5. Cut bandanna in half diagonally. (You will use only ½ of bandanna.) From Wonder-Under, cut 1 (1" x 20") strip, 1 (1") square, and 1 (1" x 22") strip. Press 1" x 20" Wonder-Under strip onto wrong side of 1 bandanna piece along cut edge. Remove paper backing.

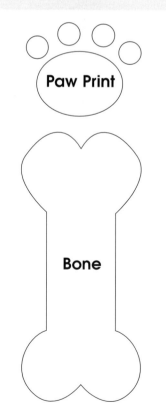

Paw Print

Bone

Fold cut edge to wrong side along inner edge of strip. Fuse. Continue folding bandanna in 1" sections until you reach point. Lift point of bandanna. Center and press 1" Wonder-Under square under point. Remove paper backing. Reposition point of bandanna and fuse to hold point in place.

6. Center and press 1" x 22" strip of Wonder-Under along back of folded bandanna. (Approximately 5" of each end of bandanna should remain free.) Remove paper backing. Position pot on its side. Place folded bandanna around rim of pot. Using tip of iron and beginning at center of bandanna, fuse bandanna to rim of pot. (You may need to fuse longer

than usual to get a strong bond.) Tie free ends of bandanna in knot.

7. To make container lid, with saucer still upside down, glue wooden ball to center of saucer (see photo). Let glue dry.

8. Fill container with doggie treats.

Fabulous Faux Fur Scarf

Create this high-fashion winter wrap without investing much time or money. This elegant accessory requires only three inexpensive materials, and you can make it in less than an hour.

Designed by Dondra G. Parham

Materials

⅓ yard 60"-wide red acrylic fleece

2 (8") squares Pellon® Heavy Duty Wonder-Under®

2 (8") squares acrylic faux leopard fur

Instructions

Note: If using synthetic fabrics, we recommend stitching the appliqué edges for added security.

1. Cut 1 (10" x 60") strip from fleece. Cut off selvages.

2. Trace 1 star onto paper side of each Wonder-Under square. Press 1 Wonder-Under square onto wrong side of each fur square, pressing for 3 seconds only.

(Acrylic fur can melt with intense heat.) Using tip of scissors, cut out stars along pattern lines, cutting through backing fabric only. Shake out stars to remove loose pieces of fur. Remove paper backing.

3. Referring to photo, position 1 star on right side of each end of fleece. Turn fleece and stars over as 1 unit. Press from wrong side of fleece to fuse stars in place. Fluff fur with fingers.

Star

Fantastic Footwear

These flashy tennis shoes are a cute finishing touch for a new outfit. Embellish the shoes with either motifs cut from printed fabrics or with appliqués of your own design.

Designed by Betsy Cooper Scott

Materials

Pellon® Heavy Duty Wonder-Under®
¼ yard fabric printed with desired motifs*
1 pair plain canvas tennis shoes
1 pair old socks
2 yards ⅜"-wide ribbon
Liquid ravel preventer
Transparent tape

* If possible, choose a fabric that has the same color background as the tennis shoes. You will not have to cut the motifs as precisely. The fabric pictured is Puddlejumpers by Hi-Fashion Fabrics Inc.

Instructions

Note: For added security, especially if shoes will be washed frequently, outline motifs with coordinating dimensional fabric paint.

1. Press Wonder-Under onto wrong side of fabric. Cut out desired motifs. Remove paper backing.

2. Stuff shoes firmly with socks. Fuse motifs onto shoes as desired.

3. Cut ribbon in half. Coat ends with liquid ravel preventer. Let dry. Using tape, roll cut ends of ribbon tightly. Lace shoes.

Other Ideas

For an adult version of this fun footwear, consider fusing polka dots or watermelon slices to slip-on canvas tennis shoes. Be sure to look through the patterns in this book for other fun motifs.

Calendar for All Seasons

Create this practical wallhanging for your calendar girl. The blank field at the top of the purchased calendar suits seasonal appliqués.

Designed by Michele Crawford

Materials

Rotary cutter, ruler, and mat
⅛ yard green check cotton fabric with stars
¾"-wide Pellon® Heavy Duty Wonder-Under® fusible tape
Purchased canvas calendar*
Hot-glue gun and glue sticks
7 (⅞"-diameter) wooden buttons
¾ yard Pellon® Heavy Duty Wonder-Under®

For Winter Block:
Fabric for appliqués: 4" x 5" piece green print, 2½" x 4" piece white print, 1½" x 1¾" piece black print, 1" x 2½" piece gold print
Dimensional fabric paints in squeeze bottles: black, orange, brown
1 snowflake button

For Spring Block:
Fabric for appliqués: 1½" square yellow print, 2½" x 4" piece tan print, 2½" x 3" piece green print, 1½" x 2" piece pink print
6" (⅛"-wide) pale blue ribbon

1 (¼"- to ½"-diameter) white pom-pom
1 ladybug button

For Summer Block:
Fabric for appliqués: 1½" square yellow print, 3" x 3½" piece white print, ½" x 4" piece brown print, 1½" x 4½" piece blue plaid
Medium blue dimensional fabric paint in squeeze bottle
1 (⅝"-diameter) red star button

For Fall Block:
Fabric for appliqués: 3" x 5" piece tan plaid, 1" x 2½" piece gold print, 2" x 2½" piece rust print, 2" x 2½" piece second rust print
Green dimensional fabric paint in squeeze bottle
1 bat button

* Calendar (4262-98) by BagWorks. See page 160 for more information.

Instructions

1. Using rotary cutter, ruler, and mat, cut 5 (¾" x 13½") strips and 2 (¾" x 23") strips from green check fabric. Press fusible tape to wrong side of strips. Remove paper backing.

2. Referring to photo, fuse 1 (13½"-long) strip down center of blank field on calendar. Fuse 1 (13½"-long) strip across top of calendar, just below casing seam line.

Fuse 1 (13½"-long) strip across center of blank field. Fuse 1 (13½"-long) strip across bottom of blank field, just above printed dates. Fuse remaining 13½"-long strip across bottom of calendar, just above seam line. Fuse 23"-long strips down sides of calendar, covering ends of previous strips.

3. Referring to photo, hot-glue wooden buttons in place at intersections of fabric strips.

4. Trace patterns onto paper side of Wonder-Under. Leaving approximate ½" margin, cut out Wonder-Under shapes. Referring to photo for colors, press shapes onto wrong side of fabric pieces. Cut out shapes along pattern lines. Remove paper backing. Referring to photograph, fuse shapes in place.

5. To complete winter block: Referring to photo, use black fabric paint to make snowman eyes, mouth, and buttons. Let dry. Use orange fabric paint to make carrot nose. Let dry. Use brown fabric paint to make stick arms. Let dry. Hot-glue snowflake button to top of tree.

6. To complete spring block: Tie ribbon in bow. Referring to photo, hot-glue bow to bunny's neck. Hot-glue pom-pom in place for tail. Hot-glue ladybug button to flower leaf.

7. To complete summer block: Referring to photo, use medium blue fabric paint to paint waves on each side of boat. Let dry. Hot-glue star button in place at top of mast.

8. To complete fall block: Referring to photo, use green fabric paint to make pumpkin stems. Let dry. Hot-glue bat button in place on haystack.

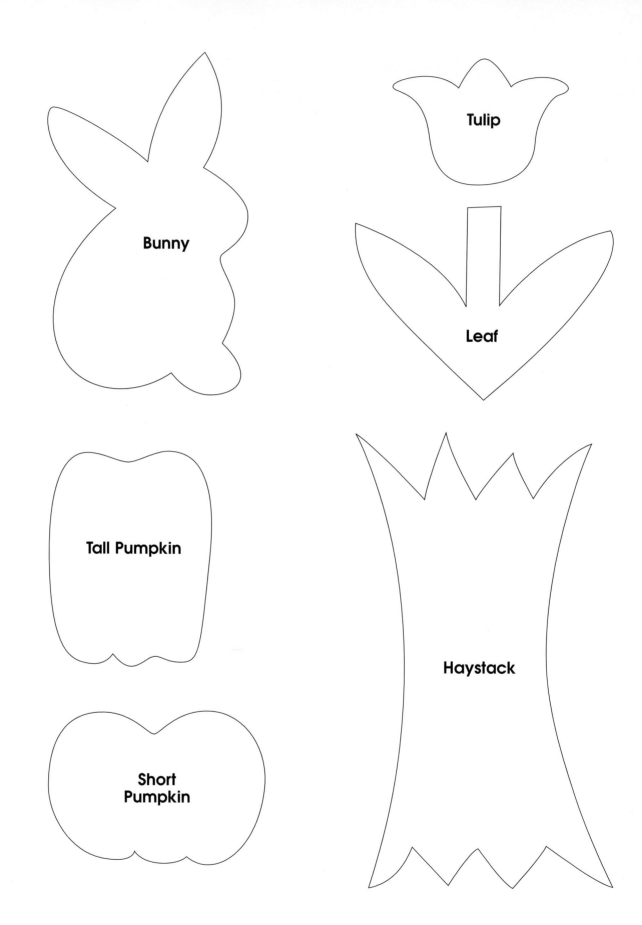

Bunny

Tulip

Leaf

Tall Pumpkin

Haystack

Short
Pumpkin

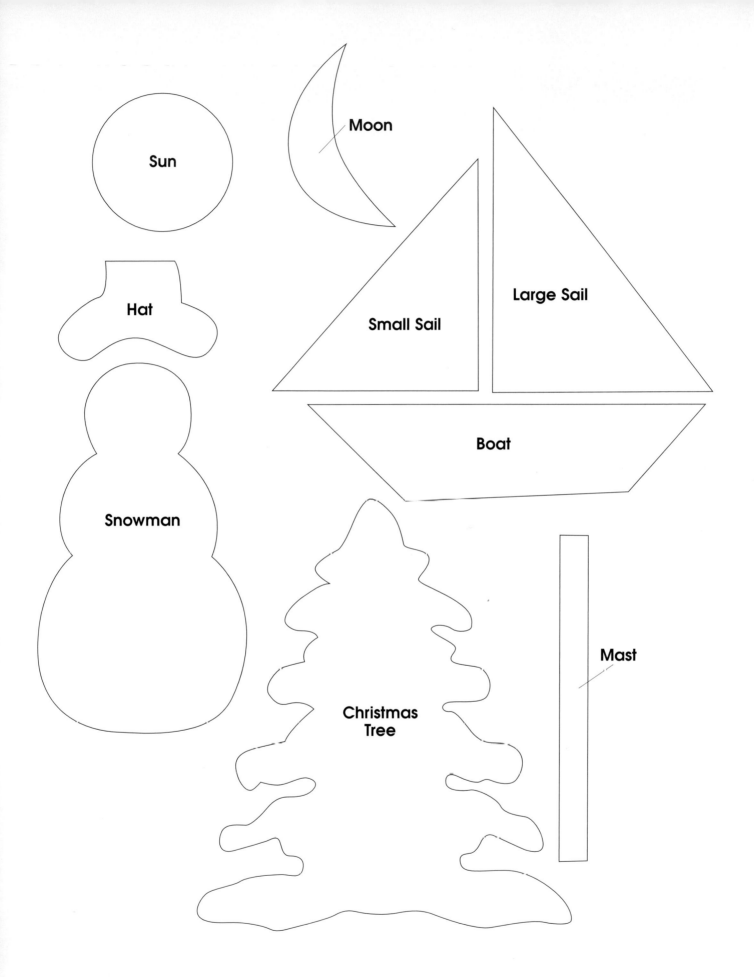

Sun

Moon

Hat

Small Sail

Large Sail

Boat

Snowman

Mast

Christmas
Tree

Housewarming Gifts

Welcome new neighbors with baked goods covered with an appliquéd bread cloth. Or honor the newcomers with a party, and bring a set of cocktail napkins for them to keep. Either way, Pellon® Wonder-Under® makes it simple for you to offer a gracious gift.

Ivy Bedding

A sheet set is a useful housewarming gift,
and a set strewn with ivy is a memorable one.

Designed by Betsy Cooper Scott

Instructions

Note: For added security, especially if sheet and pillowcase will be washed frequently, outline shapes with coordinating dimensional fabric paint.

1. Wash, dry, and iron sheet, pillowcase, and fabric. Do not use fabric softener in washer or dryer.

2. Trace desired number of leaf patterns onto paper side of Wonder-Under. Leaving approximate ½" margin, cut around Wonder-Under shapes. Press shapes onto wrong side of fabric. Cut out shapes along pattern lines. Remove paper backing.

3. Position ivy leaves on right side of flat sheet edge as desired. Fuse leaves to sheet one at a time. Repeat for pillowcase.

4. Following manufacturer's instructions, mix craft paint and textile medium. Using paintbrush and paint, add a line connecting leaves on sheet and pillowcase. Let dry. Add vein lines on each leaf. Let dry.

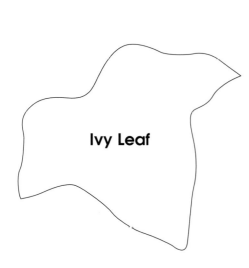

Ivy Leaf

Address Book

Purchased plain address
  book
Fabric*
Pellon® Wonder-Under®
¾"-wide ribbon*
Hot-glue gun and glue sticks

*Yardage will depend on
  size of book.

A new homeowner will have plenty of numbers to record in this fabric-wrapped address book—be sure to add your address to the book before wrapping it.

Designed by Heidi King

Instructions

1. Using opened address book as guide, cut fabric 2" larger than book on all sides. Cut Wonder-Under to fit fabric rectangle. Press Wonder-Under onto wrong side of fabric. Remove paper backing.

2. Fuse fabric to surface of address book, starting at 1 edge. Turn edges to inside of book and fuse in place.

3. Cut ribbon in half. Hot-glue 1 end of 1 piece to inside of book front cover. Using remaining ribbon, repeat for inside back cover. Tie ribbon into bow to close.

Other Ideas

If using solid fabrics, decorate the covered book with appliquéd motifs, buttons, lace, or dimensional fabric paint. Personalize the book with a painted or appliquéd address, a name, or a phone number on the front cover.

Cocktail Napkins

Give a gift of style. Make a set of napkins with
sophisticated flair or subtle elegance.

Designed by Dondra G. Parham

Materials
(for 4 napkins)

⅛ yard each 4 washable
   linen-blend fabrics
Rotary cutter with 1 straight
   blade, 1 wave blade,
   and mat
Ruler
¾"-wide Pellon® Wonder-
   Under® fusible tape
Textile medium
Gold acrylic craft paint
Fine-tip paintbrush

Instructions

1. Wash, dry, and iron fabrics. Do not use fabric softener in washer or dryer.

2. With straight blade in rotary cutter, and following measurements below, cut 1 A, 1 B, 1 C, and 1 D from each fabric. Stack same size shapes together.

3. Select 1 A, 1 B, 1 C, and 1 D piece from each color. Press Wonder-Under tape onto right side of 1 short edge of A and B pieces.

With wave blade in rotary cutter, cut Wonder-Under edges (Diagram A). Remove paper backing. Cut 1 short edge of C and D pieces. Fuse wavy edge of piece C onto corresponding edge of piece A (Diagram B). Repeat for pieces B and D. Press Wonder-Under tape onto right side of 1 long edge of unit A/C. Cut Wonder-Under edge of unit A/C and 1 long edge of unit B/D (Diagram C). Remove paper backing. Fuse wavy edge of unit B/D to wavy edge of unit A/C, aligning intersecting points (Diagram D).

4. With straight blade in rotary cutter and using ruler, trim napkin edges to 6" x 9".

5. Following manufacturer's instructions, mix textile medium with craft paint. Using paintbrush and paint, apply ¼"-wide line to napkin edges. Let dry. Repeat steps 3 through 5 to make remaining napkins.

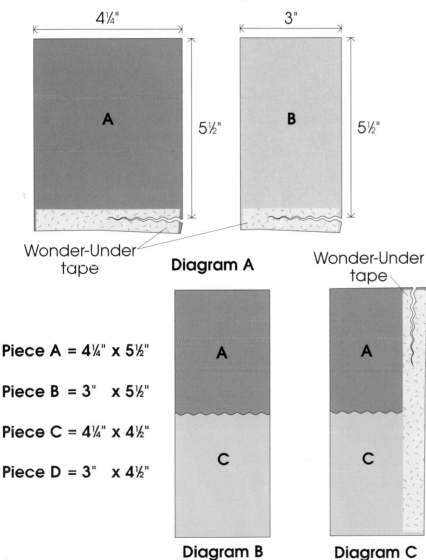

Wonder-Under tape

Diagram A

Piece A = 4¼" x 5½"

Piece B = 3" x 5½"

Piece C = 4¼" x 4½"

Piece D = 3" x 4½"

Diagram B

Wonder-Under tape

Diagram C

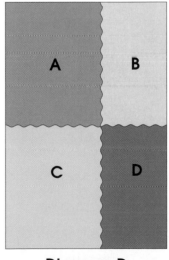

Diagram D

Picnicking with the Ants

Materials

Purchased tablecloth and
napkins
Assorted fabric scraps for
appliqués: black, blue
Pellon® Heavy Duty
Wonder-Under®
Dimensional fabric paints in
squeeze bottles: black,
white, blue, red
Fine-tip white permanent
fabric marker

It's the only place you'll see ants welcome at a picnic. Use the ant appliqués to embellish a picnic basket to go with the set.

Designed by Phyllis Dunstan

Instructions

1. Wash, dry, and iron table-cloth, napkins, and fabrics. Do not use fabric softener in washer or dryer.

2. Trace desired number of patterns from page 56 onto paper side of Wonder-Under. *(Note:* Number of ants and shoes will depend on size of tablecloth.) Leaving approximate ½" margin, cut around Wonder-Under shapes. Referring to photo for colors, press shapes onto wrong side of fabrics. Cut out shapes along pattern lines. Remove paper backing.

3. Arrange ants and shoes along edges of tablecloth. Fuse shapes into place. Fuse ant and shoes to 1 corner of each napkin.

4. Using dimensional fabric paints, draw legs, antennae, body segment lines, mouth, and shoe outlines. Let dry after each application. Using white marker, draw ant's eye. Finish eye with dot of black dimensional fabric paint. Let dry. Repeat on remaining ants.

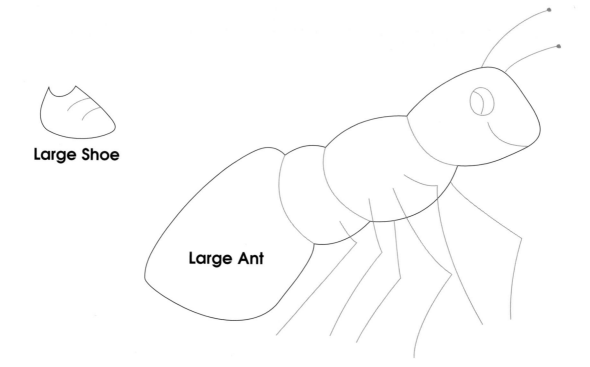

Large Shoe

Large Ant

Gray lines are painted lines.

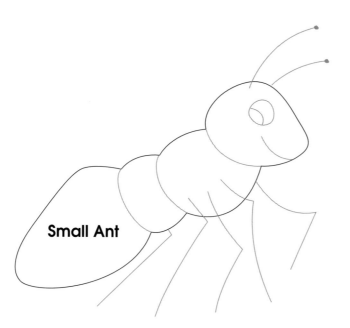

Small Shoe

Small Ant

Shower Curtain

Display your genius for design. Jazz up a plain shower curtain
with simple shapes and cool colors.

Designed by Betsy Cooper Scott

Materials

Purchased plain cotton or
  polyester fabric shower
  curtain
Fabric for appliqués: ½ yard
  each pink, yellow, blue,
  green
Pellon® Heavy Duty
  Wonder-Under®

Instructions

Note: For added security,
especially if shower curtain
will be washed frequently,
outline shapes with coordinating dimensional fabric
paint.

1. Wash, dry, and iron curtain and fabrics. Do not use
fabric softener in washer or
dryer.

2. Trace desired number of
patterns onto paper side of
Wonder-Under. Leaving
approximate ½" margin, cut
around Wonder-Under
shapes. Referring to photo
for colors, press shapes onto
wrong side of fabrics. Cut
out shapes along pattern
lines. Remove paper
backing.

3. Arrange shapes on shower
curtain as desired. Fuse
shapes to curtain one at a
time.

Other Ideas

Shower curtains can be changed with each
season. Experiment with colorful solid and
painted fabrics using the geometric patterns
provided. Or use other patterns in this book,
such as the ivy leaf on page 49 or the
hydrangea bloom on page 62, to coordinate
with your home decor.

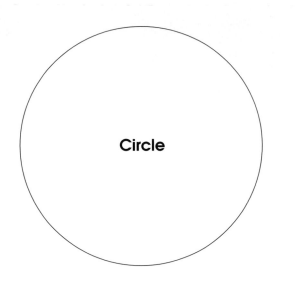

Circle

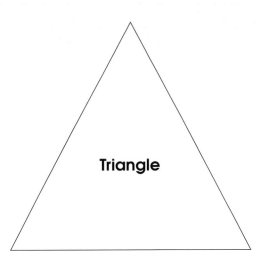

Triangle

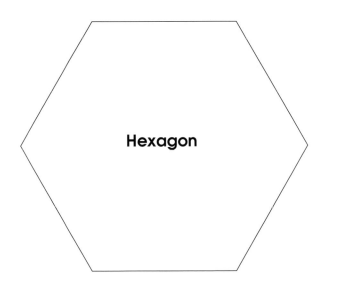

Hexagon

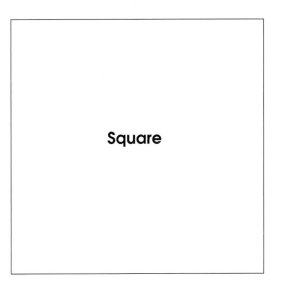

Square

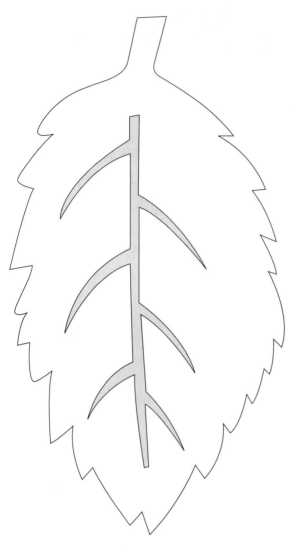

Cut out shaded areas.

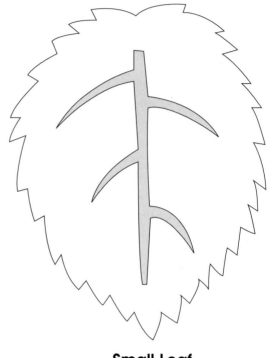

Small Leaf

Large Leaf

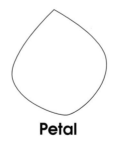

Petal

Wine Bottle Cover

Celebrate your new neighbor's arrival with a warm hello
and a bottle of wine or sparkling water in a decorated gift bag.

Designed by Betsy Cooper Scott

Materials

Pellon® Wonder-Under®
Fabric scraps for appliqués:
  purple, green
Purchased plain wine bottle
  cover with tie

Instructions

1. Trace 3 small grapes, 7 medium grapes, 3 large grapes, 1 stem, 1 leaf, and 1 leaf reversed onto paper side of Wonder-Under. Leaving approximate ½" margin, cut around Wonder-Under shapes. Referring to photo for colors, press shapes onto wrong side of fabric. Cut out shapes along pattern lines. Remove paper backing.

2. Referring to photo, fuse grapes, leaves, and stem onto wine bottle cover.

Other Ideas

You can personalize the wine bottle cover with a monogram or an appliqué of a house.

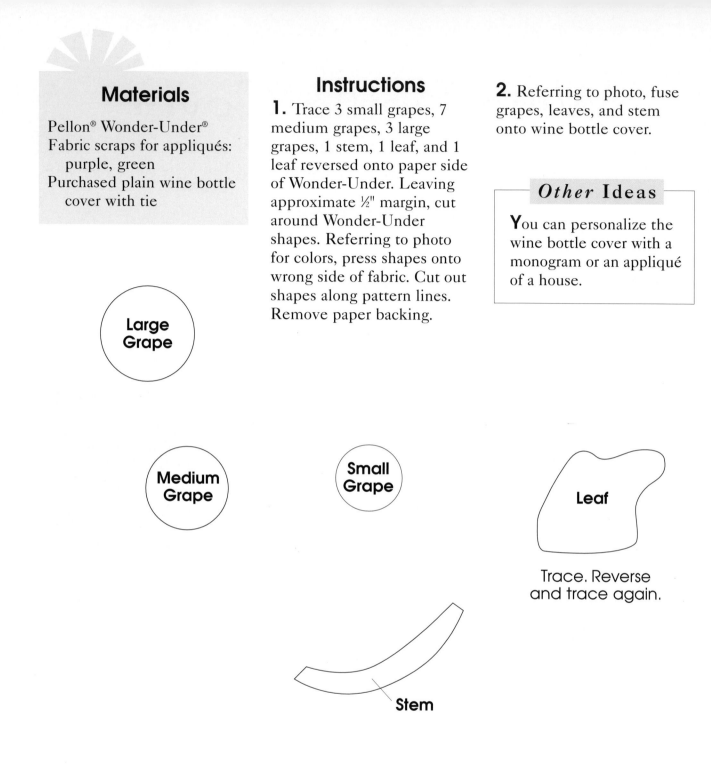

Large
Grape

Medium
Grape

Small
Grape

Leaf

Trace. Reverse
and trace again.

Stem

Fridge Magnets

Materials

For both:
Pellon® Wonder-Under®
Fabric scraps for appliqués
Thin cardboard
Hot-glue gun and glue sticks
Magnet strips

For Cat:
2 (10-mm) wiggle eyes

For Teapot:
Pink dimensional fabric
    paint in squeeze bottle
5 blue seed beads

For Heart:
1 crocheted doily
1 novelty button
1 bow with pearl center

Instructions for Cat

1. Trace 2 cats and 1 scarf from page 66 onto paper side of Wonder-Under. Leaving approximate ½" margin, cut around Wonder-Under shapes. Referring to photo for colors, press shapes onto wrong side of fabrics. Cut out shapes along pattern lines. Remove paper backing.

2. Using removed paper backing as guide, trace 1 cat on cardboard. Cut out. Stack the following pieces: 1 cat, Wonder-Under side up; cardboard piece; and 1 cat, right side up. Fuse pieces together. Flip over stack, and fuse from other side.

Trace your cookie cutters or our patterns to make these simply charming refrigerator accessories.

Designed by Nancy Worrell

3. Fuse scarf on 1 side of cat. Glue eyes on cat using hot glue.

4. Cut 1" of magnet from strip. Hot-glue strip to back of cat.

Instructions for Teapot

1. Follow Steps 1 and 2 of cat instructions, using teapot pattern.

2. Using dimensional fabric paint and following pattern lines, embellish teapot. While paint is wet, add seed beads to center of painted stars on teapot. Let dry. To finish, follow Step 4 of cat instructions.

Instructions for Heart

1. Follow Steps 1 and 2 of cat instructions, using heart pattern.

2. Hot-glue doily, button, and bow to 1 side of heart. To finish, follow Step 4 of cat instructions.

Other Ideas

This project is great for making batches of magnets for fairs and fundraisers.

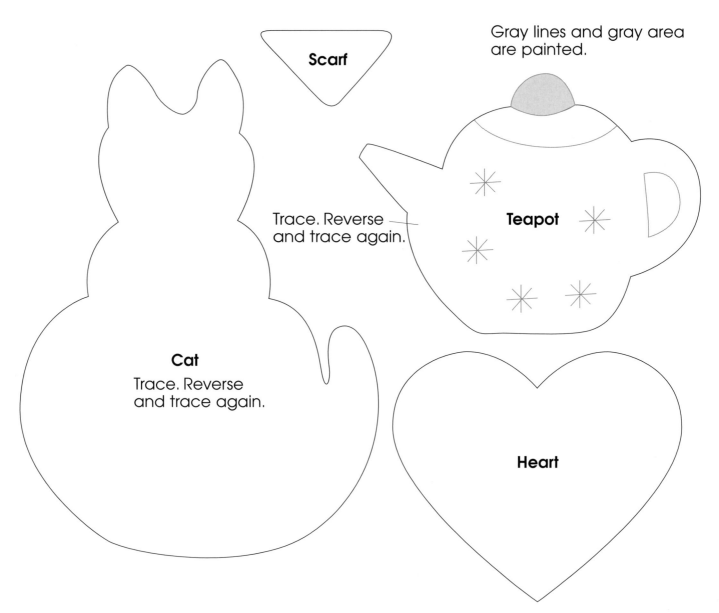

Scarf

Trace. Reverse and trace again.

Gray lines and gray area are painted.

Teapot

Cat
Trace. Reverse and trace again.

Heart

Signature Sheet Set

Warm up a guest room with words of welcome. These customized sheets make a lovely gift, but you might want to keep them to welcome your own guests.

Designed By Dondra G. Parham

Materials

Purchased plain flat sheet
and pillowcase
Fabrics for appliqués: black,
large-printed motif*
Textile medium
Acrylic craft paints: gold,
black (optional)
Paintbrushes: wide-tip, fine-
tip (optional)
Pellon® Wonder-Under®

*Yardage will depend on
size of sheet.

Instructions

Note: For added security,
especially if sheet and pillowcase will be washed frequently, outline lettering
and motifs with coordinating
dimensional fabric paint.

1. Wash, dry, and iron sheet,
pillowcase, and fabrics. Do
not use fabric softener in
washer or dryer.

2. Following manufacturer's
instructions, mix textile
medium with gold craft
paint. Using wide-tip paintbrush, paint top edge of flat
sheet and opening edge of
pillowcase. Let dry.

3. Trace patterns provided,
hand-write, or use home
computer to create printed
saying. *(Note:* A copy center
will reverse type for use
with Wonder-Under and can
enlarge type to desired size.)
The sheet pictured bears
the saying "The ornament
of a house is the guests who
frequent it." Trace lettering
onto paper side of Wonder-
Under. Press Wonder-Under
onto wrong side of black
fabric. Cut out lettering on
pattern lines. Remove paper
backing.

4. Position lettering across
painted edge of flat sheet, as
desired. Fuse lettering to
sheet.

5. Press Wonder-Under onto
wrong side of large-print
fabric. Cut out desired
motifs close to edges.
Position motifs along edges
of sheet and pillowcase.
Fuse motifs onto sheet and
pillowcase one at a time.

6. Following manufacturer's
instructions, mix textile
medium with black craft
paint. Using fine-tip paintbrush and paint, add stems
and details to motifs if
desired. Let dry.

Other Ideas

Instead of fusing letters to the
sheet, use dimensional fabric
paint to write on the sheet and
pillowcase. Your library should
have a good selection of decorative lettering books to choose
from.

The ornament of a house is the guests who frequent it.

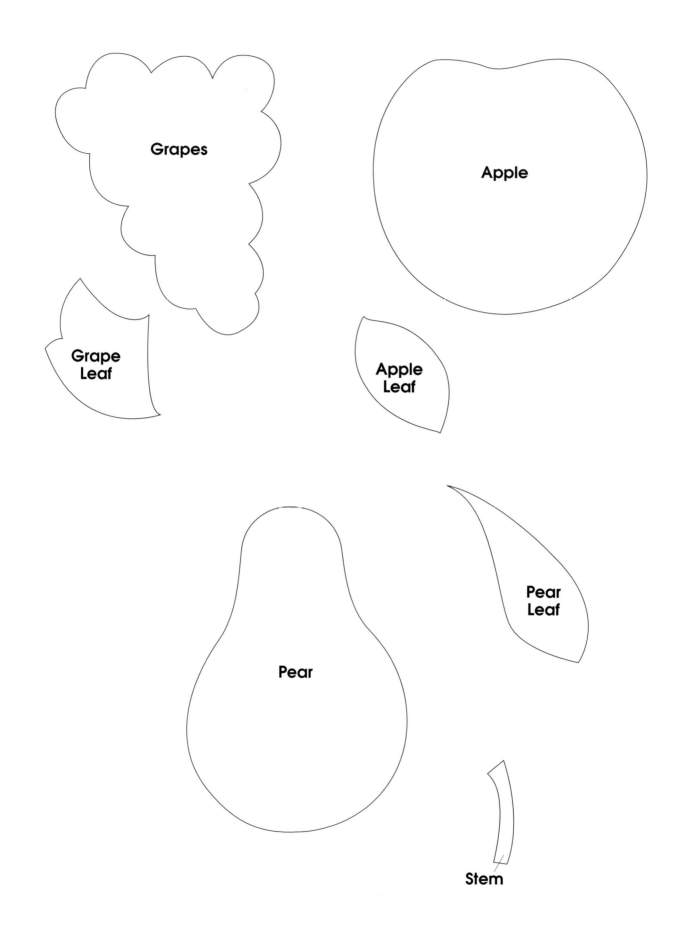

Grapes

Apple

Grape
Leaf

Apple
Leaf

Pear
Leaf

Pear

Stem

Coffee Time Apron & Potholder

These trendy kitchen accessories make an appropriate gift
for a man or a woman.

Designed by Cynthia Moody Wheeler

Materials
(for 1 apron and 1 potholder)

Purchased plain apron and potholder
Assorted fabric scraps for appliqués (at least 4" square): novelty black-and-white prints
Pellon® Heavy Duty Wonder-Under®
Black dimensional fabric paint in squeeze bottle
Wide-tip permanent black fabric marker (optional)

Instructions

1. Wash, dry, and iron apron, potholder, and fabrics. Do not use fabric softener in washer or dryer.

2. Trace 4 cups, 4 saucers, 4 inner cups, and 8 steam patterns onto paper side of Wonder-Under. Leaving approximate ½" margin, cut around Wonder-Under shapes. Referring to photo, press shapes onto wrong side of fabrics. Cut out shapes along pattern lines. Remove paper backing.

3. Position and fuse saucer, cup, inner cup, and steam in that order, on front of apron. Repeat for remaining cups on apron and potholder. Outline each appliqué with dimensional fabric paint. Let dry.

4. Using marker, draw a ¼"-wide line around apron top and pocket, if desired. For similar effect on potholder, outline holder with dimensional fabric paint. Let dry.

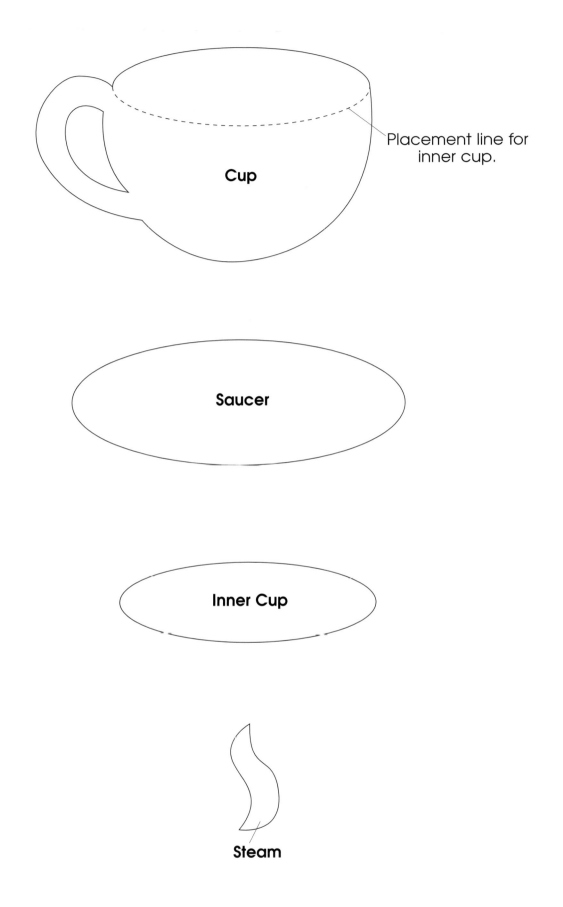

Cup

Placement line for inner cup.

Saucer

Inner Cup

Steam

Bread Covers

Homemade bread is a traditional housewarming gift. Dress a loaf with an appliquéd cloth, and you'll give two gifts in one.

Designed by Lois Winston

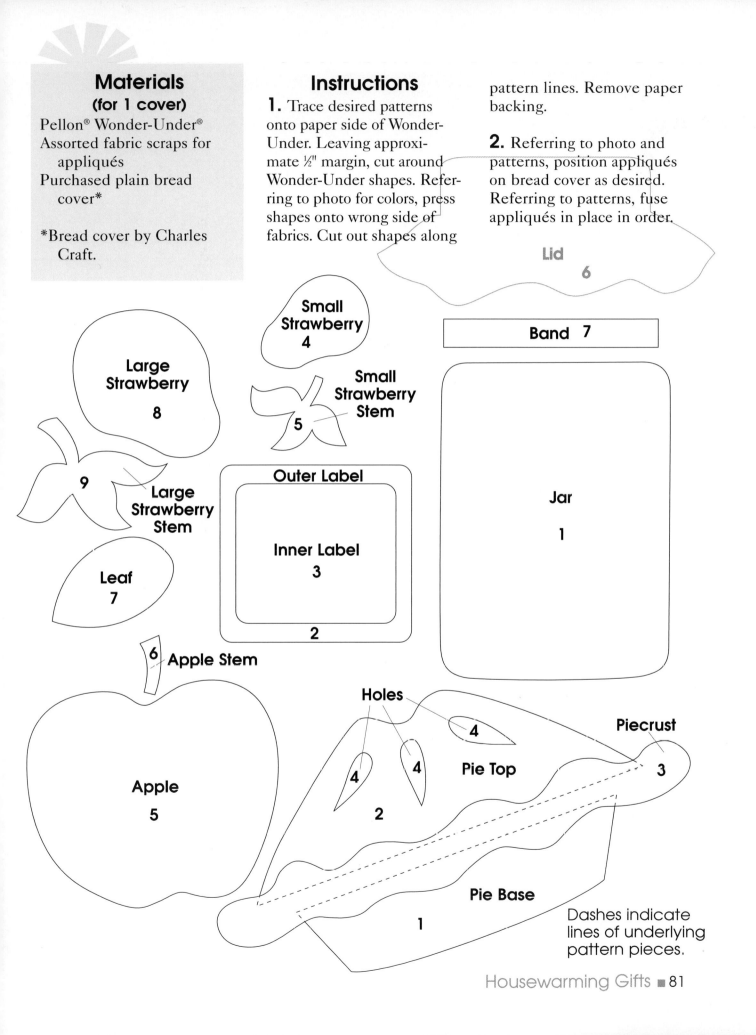

Materials
(for 1 cover)
Pellon® Wonder-Under®
Assorted fabric scraps for
 appliqués
Purchased plain bread
 cover*

*Bread cover by Charles
Craft.

Instructions
1. Trace desired patterns
onto paper side of Wonder-
Under. Leaving approxi-
mate ½" margin, cut around
Wonder-Under shapes. Referring to photo for colors, press
shapes onto wrong side of
fabrics. Cut out shapes along
pattern lines. Remove paper
backing.

2. Referring to photo and
patterns, position appliqués
on bread cover as desired.
Referring to patterns, fuse
appliqués in place in order.

Lid
6

Band 7

Jar
1

Small
Strawberry
4

Small
Strawberry
Stem
5

Large
Strawberry
8

Large
Strawberry
Stem
9

Leaf
7

Outer Label

Inner Label
3

2

6 Apple Stem

Apple
5

Holes

Piecrust

Pie Top
4

4

4

2

3

Pie Base
1

Dashes indicate
lines of underlying
pattern pieces.

Throw Pillows

Embellish plain pillows with fancy fabric appliqués. The friend who receives them will never guess how simple they were to create.

Designed by Betsy Cooper Scott

Materials
(for 1 pillow)

Pellon® Heavy Duty
  Wonder-Under®
Fabric with large motif for
  appliqué*
Purchased plain pillow**

*Yardage will depend on
  fabric choice. The fabric
  pictured is Hillhouse/Multi
  by Kaufman.
**We used a 16" x 16"
  pillow.

Instructions

1. Press Wonder-Under onto wrong side of fabric. Cut out motif as close to edges as possible. Remove paper backing.

2. Center motif on pillow front. Starting from outer edge of design, fuse motif onto pillow.

Other Ideas

Embellishing large items is easier when you use fabrics printed with large motifs. Use this simple technique to finish a pair of plain curtains to match your throw pillows. Or create custom drapes, bedding, and shower curtains.

Bride's Memory Book

Help the bride keep track of all the planning and parties with a lacy covered binder.

Designed by Betsy Cooper Scott

♥ ♥ ♥ ♥ ♥ ♥ ♥ ♥ ♥ ♥ ♥ ♥ ♥ ♥ ♥ ♥ ♥ ♥ ♥ ♥

Materials

3-ring binder or album
1 yard bridal fabric
½ yard lace fabric
Pellon® Heavy Duty
　Wonder-Under®
¾"-wide Pellon® Wonder-
　Under® fusible tape
5 yards ⅛"-wide ribbon
Large-eyed hand needle
3 yards 1½"-wide gathered
　lace with eyelet edging
2 (4"-diameter) lace or
　crocheted heart-shaped
　appliqués

Instructions

1. Using binder or album as guide, cut bridal fabric 2" beyond all edges of binder. Using same guide, cut lace fabric 1" beyond all edges of binder.

2. Cut Wonder-Under to fit bridal fabric piece. Press onto wrong side of bridal fabric. Remove paper backing.

3. Fuse bridal fabric onto binder. Open binder and fuse edges of fabric to inside. Press Wonder-Under tape onto edges of lace fabric. Remove paper backing. With lace piece flat and binder open on top of lace, fuse edges of lace to inside of binder over bridal fabric.

4. Thread ribbon through large-eyed needle. Knot 1 end. Referring to photo, and starting at binder's spine, weave ribbon through eyelet edge of gathered lace and through lace fabric on edge of binder. Continue weaving ribbon in this manner around edges of binder. Overlap lace at end, and tie knot and bow with ribbon ends. Trim ribbon.

5. Cut 2 (3") squares from Wonder-Under. Press 1 square onto wrong side of lace appliqué. Remove paper backing. Referring to photo, position and fuse lace appliqué onto front of binder. Weave ribbon through top center of heart. Tie bow, knot and trim ends. Repeat for remaining appliqué.

6. To finish inside of binder, cut bridal fabric ¼" smaller around all edges of binder front cover. Repeat for back cover. Cut Wonder-Under to fit fabric pieces. Press Wonder-Under onto fabric pieces. Remove paper backings. Fuse bridal fabric to inside, covering lace and bridal fabric edges.

Wedding Memories

Wedding Keepsake Boxes

Materials

For Box:
Purchased plain wooden box
Fine-grit sandpaper
Acrylic craft paint
Paintbrush
Pellon® Heavy Duty
   Wonder-Under®
Fabric scrap (yardage will
   depend on size of box)
Craft knife

For Video Cassette Case:
Pellon® Heavy Duty
   Wonder-Under®
½ yard fabric
2 cardboard video cassette
   cases
Towel

Give the bride and groom a storage set that will hold the sentimental treasures saved from their big day.

Designed by Heidi King

♥ ♥ ♥ ♥ ♥ ♥ ♥ ♥ ♥ ♥ ♥ ♥ ♥ ♥ ♥ ♥ ♥ ♥ ♥

Instructions for Box

1. Sand box lightly with sandpaper. Remove all dust. Using paintbrush and craft paint, paint all surfaces of box. Let dry.

2. Press Wonder-Under onto wrong side of fabric scrap. Remove paper backing. Fuse fabric onto all sides of center portion of wooden box. (You may need to fuse longer than usual to get a strong bond.) Using craft knife, trim fabric to fit along edges of box.

Instructions for Video Cassette Case

1. Press Wonder-Under onto wrong side of fabric.

2. To make pattern, carefully take apart 1 cardboard cassette case. Trace pattern onto Wonder-Under side of fabric. Cut along pattern lines. Remove paper backing.

3. Fold towel into small rectangle. Stuff towel into remaining cassette case to act as pressing surface. Fuse fabric onto remaining case.

Cutwork Tray Mat

Pellon® Wonder-Under® helps you simulate the beauty of cutwork, without the time-consuming effort. This mat makes an elegant liner for the newlyweds' breakfast tray.

Designed by Françoise Dudal Kirkman

Materials

½ yard linen
Tracing paper
Pellon® Heavy Duty
    Wonder-Under®
Cutting mat
Craft knife with extra blades

Instructions

1. Wash, dry, and iron fabric. Do not use fabric softener in washer or dryer.

2. Trace pattern onto tracing paper. Cut 2 rectangles of linen to fit pattern. Press Wonder-Under onto wrong side of 1 linen rectangle. Remove paper backing. Fuse rectangle onto wrong side of remaining rectangle.

3. Place tracing paper pattern on fused linen rectangle and use scissors to cut decorative edge. Place linen rectangle and paper pattern on cutting mat. Use craft knife to cut interior details from linen. Change knife blades as needed.

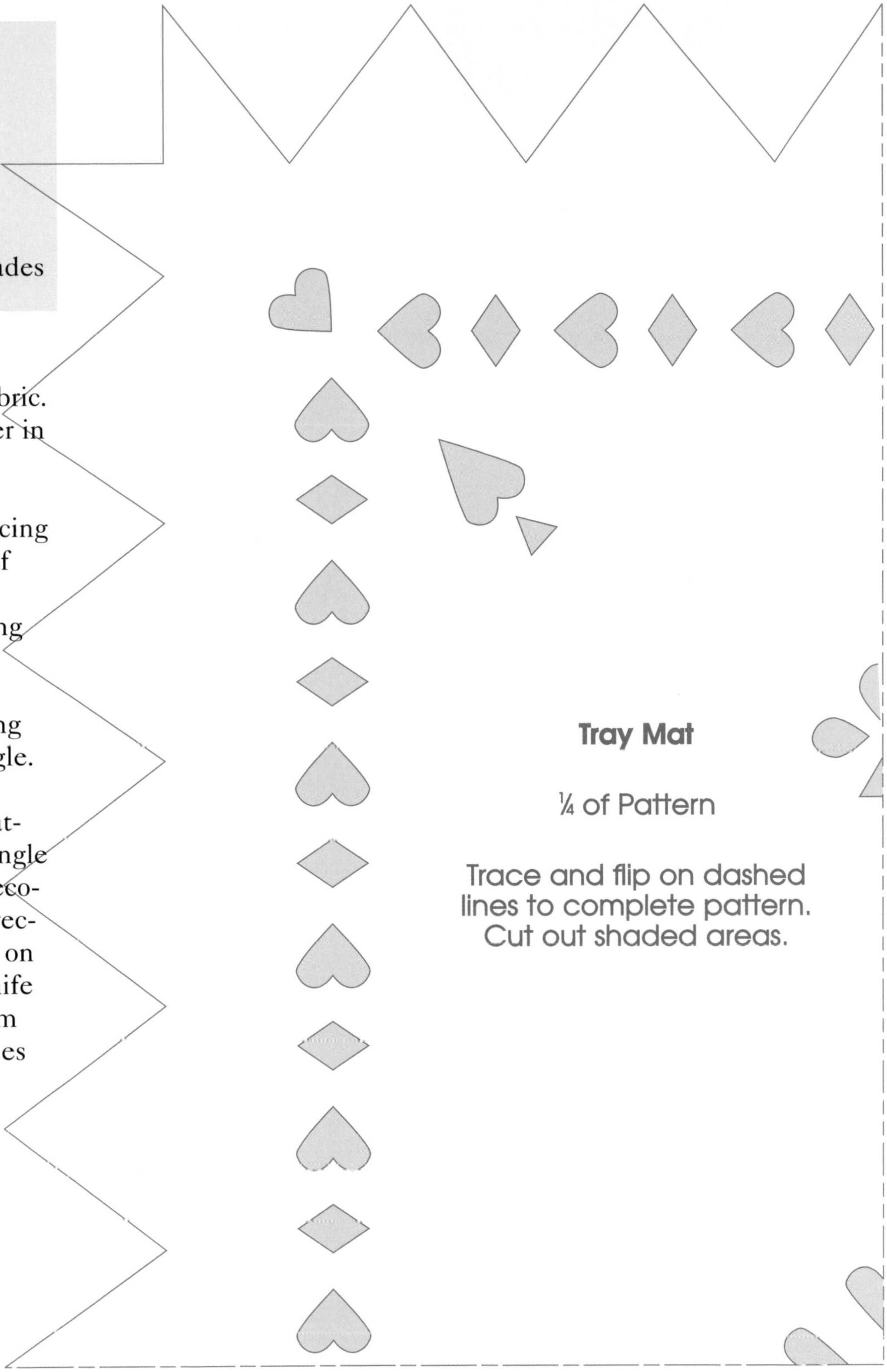

Tray Mat

¼ of Pattern

Trace and flip on dashed lines to complete pattern. Cut out shaded areas.

Scented Sachets

Materials
(for 1 sachet)

Contrasting fabric scraps
  (at least 8" square)
¾"-wide Pellon® Wonder-
  Under® fusible tape
Potpourri or essential oil
9" square lightweight batting
⅓ yard (⅛"-wide) ribbon
1 (½"-diameter) bead

These stylish sachets make thoughtful mementos for bridesmaids. They'll love the sweet scent that fills their closet.

Designed by Dondra G. Parham

♥ ♥ ♥ ♥ ♥ ♥ ♥ ♥ ♥ ♥ ♥ ♥ ♥ ♥ ♥ ♥ ♥ ♥ ♥ ♥

Instructions

1. From contrasting fabric scraps, cut 1 (6" x 8") piece for sachet body and 1 (6" x 4") piece for accent. Press Wonder-Under tape onto right side of 1 (6") edge of accent piece. Remove paper backing. With right sides together and raw edges aligned, fuse 1 (6") edge of sachet body fabric to accent piece. Turn right side out.

2. Cut 1 (10"-long) strip from Wonder-Under tape. Cut strip in half lengthwise. Press 1 Wonder-Under strip onto right side of 1 long edge of sachet. Remove paper backing. With right sides facing and raw edges aligned, fold sachet in half lengthwise. Fuse raw edges together. Turn tube right side out.

3. Cut 2 (2"-long) strips from Wonder-Under tape. Fold bottom edges of sachet under ½". Press 1 Wonder-Under strip onto 1 side of inside edge. Remove paper backing. Fuse folded bottom edges together.

4. Sprinkle potpourri or essential oil onto batting. Roll batting into tube the size of sachet. Slide batting into sachet. Fold top edges under ½". Press remaining 2"-long Wonder-Under strip onto 1 side of inside edge. Remove paper backing. Fold ribbon in half to form loop. Thread bead onto ribbon. Slip ribbon ends into sachet. Fuse folded top edges together, sandwiching ribbon between sachet edges.

Lovely Linens Press

Materials

1½ yards fabric
Pellon® Wonder-Under®
2 (21"-square) pieces heavyweight cardboard
2 yards (2"-wide) ribbon

This quick but beautiful present will help the bride keep her new linens safe and smooth.

Designed by Carol Tipton

❤ ❤ ❤ ❤ ❤ ❤ ❤ ❤ ❤ ❤ ❤ ❤ ❤ ❤ ❤ ❤ ❤ ❤

Instructions

1. From fabric, cut 2 (24") squares and 2 (20") squares. Press Wonder-Under onto wrong side of each square. Remove paper backing.

2. Center and fuse 1 (24") fabric square to 1 cardboard square. Turn cardboard over. Referring to Diagram, cut notches at corners of fabric square. Wrap and fuse edges of fabric onto cardboard. Repeat for remaining cardboard square.

3. Fuse 1 (20") fabric square onto unfinished side of 1 cardboard square, covering all folded edges from Step 2. Repeat for remaining square.

4. Sandwich linens between 2 fabric-covered squares. Tie ribbon around squares.

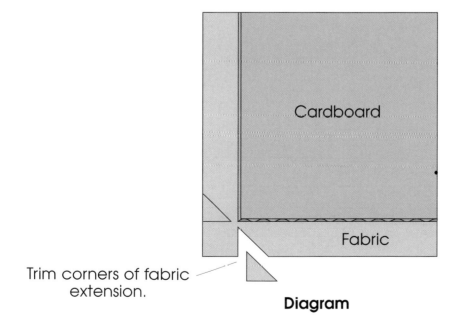

Trim corners of fabric extension.

Cardboard

Fabric

Diagram

Bridal Memories Set

A picture frame and a guest book are essential to the bride and groom. Surprise the happy couple with a customized set made in their wedding colors.

Designed by Françoise Dudal Kirkman

Materials

For both:
Pellon® Heavy Duty
   Wonder-Under®
Bridal fabric*
Handmade paper
Fabric glue
Gold metallic thread
Assorted charms or buttons
Decorative braid or trim
Hot-glue gun and glue sticks

For Frame:
Purchased (10" x 12") flat-
   faced wooden frame

For Guest Book:
⅛"-thick cardboard
Craft knife
Straight-edge ruler
Drill with ⅛"-diameter bit
Cotton embroidery floss
Assorted hand needles
   (optional)
9" x 12" pad of drawing or
   watercolor paper
Decorative paper
Rubber bands or clamps

*Yardage will depend on
   size of each project.

Instructions for Frame

1. Press Wonder-Under onto wrong side of bridal fabric. Position front of frame on paper side of bridal fabric. Using frame as guide and referring to Diagram, cut fabric piece that extends approximately 1" beyond each edge of frame. Cut notches at outer corners. Clip inner corners.

2. To decorate fabric, tear pieces of handmade paper into shapes as desired. Using fabric glue, glue pieces onto right side of fabric. Remove paper backing.

3. Center and fuse fabric on front of frame. Turn frame over. Wrap cut edges of fabric to back of frame and fuse. *(Note:* If necessary, gather fabric at outside corners of frame and use hot glue to secure.)

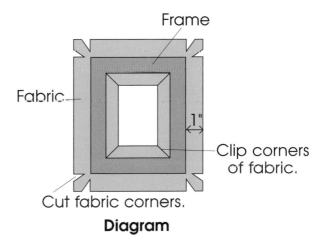

Frame

Fabric

1"

Clip corners
of fabric.

Cut fabric corners.

Diagram

4. Wrap button holes or charm rings with metallic thread. Hot-glue buttons or charms to frame front. Hot-glue decorative trim around sides of frame.

Instructions for Guest Book

1. Referring to Diagram A, cut cardboard into 2 (9½" x 12¼") rectangles. Using craft knife and straight edge, score a line 1½" from short edge of rectangle (Diagram A). Do not cut through cardboard. Repeat for other rectangle. Referring to Diagram B, cut additional cardboard into 1 (9" x 1½") piece and 1 (9" x 10¾") piece. Repeat to make 1 more set.

2. Using cardboard pieces from Diagram A as guides, cut bridal fabric to fit, leaving 1" around all edges. Press Wonder-Under onto wrong sides of both cut fabric pieces. To decorate, tear handmade paper into shapes as desired. Using fabric glue, glue shapes onto right side of fabric. Remove paper backings. Fuse fabric onto outside of both 9½" x 12¼" pieces, making sure hinges are on inside. Turn pieces over. Wrap cut edges of fabric to back of cardboard pieces and fuse. *(Note:* If necessary, gather fabric at corners and secure with glue.)

3. Using cardboard pieces cut from Diagram B, cut decorative paper or bridal fabric to fit, leaving 1" around all edges. Press Wonder-Under onto wrong sides of fabric or paper pieces. Remove paper backing. Fuse fabric or paper onto cardboard pieces. Turn pieces over. Wrap cut edges of fabric or paper onto back of cardboard and fuse.

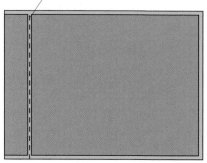

Score line.

Diagram C

4. Referring to Diagram C, hot-glue 2 pieces from Diagram B onto larger rectangle. Glue both sections to fit on either side of hinge, leaving room to bend large rectangle. Repeat for remaining pieces and rectangle.

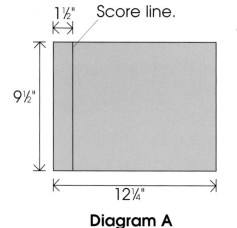

1½"   Score line.

9½"

12¼"

Diagram A

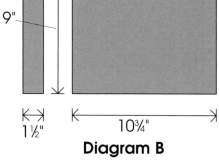

9"

1½"   10¾"

Diagram B

5. Remove cardboard backing and paper cover from paper pad. Stack album components in the following order: 1 cover, decorative side down; pad of paper, glued edges at left; and remaining cover, decorative side up. Use rubber bands or clamps to hold stack together, keeping edges even. Using drill with ⅛"-diameter bit, drill 12 equidistant holes ½" from hinged edge, drilling through all thicknesses. Using needle and embroidery floss, thread floss through holes (Diagram D). Tie knot at end. Trim ends.

6. Using hot-glue gun and referring to Diagram E, glue decorative braid or trim over hinge on outside cover. Fold trim ends to inside and glue in place. Wrap button holes or charm rings with thread. Hot-glue buttons or charms to book front.

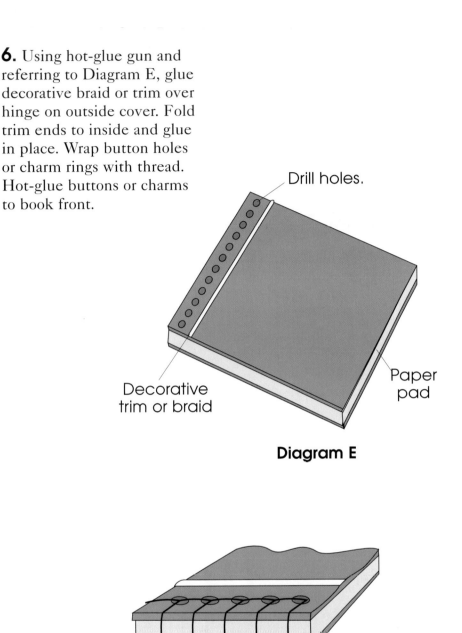

Drill holes.

Decorative trim or braid

Paper pad

Diagram E

Embroidery floss

Diagram D

Side view

3. Trace 1 star balloon, 1 round balloon, and 1 heart balloon onto paper side of Wonder-Under. Leaving approximate ½" margin, cut around Wonder-Under shapes. Press shapes onto wrong side of 3 different fabric scraps. Cut out shapes along pattern lines. Remove

paper backing. Fuse shapes to card stock. Cut out. Position and hot-glue shapes to top left-hand corner of covered mat.

4. Cut ribbon into 3 equal lengths. Starting at 1 end, make 2 loops to simulate bow. Hot-glue loops in place

at base of 1 balloon, leaving long end to hang down side of frame. Hot-glue ribbon end in place. Repeat for remaining ribbon and balloons.

5. With edges aligned, hot-glue covered mat to front of acrylic frame.

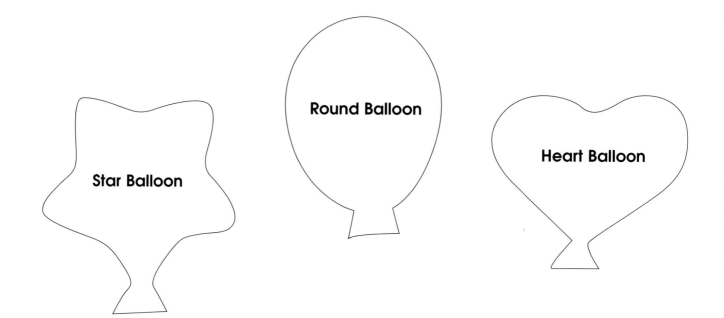

Star Balloon

Round Balloon

Heart Balloon

Noah's Ark Baby Bibs

Pellon® Wonder-Under® helps make these bibs practical
as well as educational, when baby begins to talk.

Designed by Carol Tipton

Material
(for 1 bib)

Pellon® Heavy Duty
    Wonder-Under®
Fabric scraps for appliqués
Purchased plain bib
Permanent black fabric
    marker

Instructions

Note: For added security, especially if bibs will be washed frequently, outline motifs with coordinating dimensional fabric paint.

1. Trace 2 elephants, 2 arcs, 2 giraffes, and 2 zebras (1 in reverse) onto paper side of Wonder-Under. Leaving approximate ½" margin, cut around Wonder-Under shapes. Press shapes onto wrong side of fabric scraps. Cut out shapes along pattern lines. Remove paper backing. Position and fuse pieces onto front of bib.

2. Using fabric marker, make short dashed lines around appliqués to resemble sewn stitches.

Other Ideas

Personalize a bib with baby's name or age. Create several bibs with letters of the alphabet or numbers, using bright colors to make mealtimes more fun.

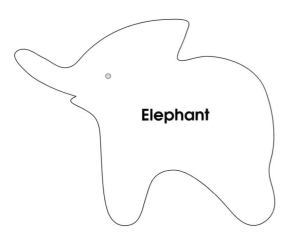

Elephant

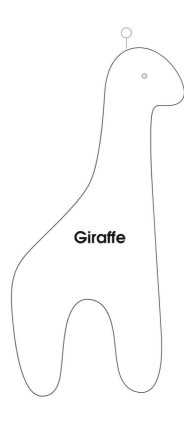

Giraffe

Shaded areas and gray lines are drawn.

Dashes indicate lines of underlying
pattern pieces.

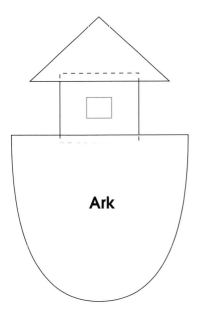

Ark

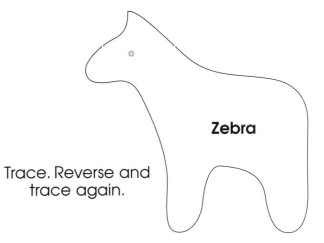

Zebra

Trace. Reverse and
trace again.

Bye, Bye Balloons Light-Switch Cover

Materials

Pellon® Wonder-Under®
Fabric scraps for appliqués
Wooden light-switch plate
Dimensional craft paint
Spray-on clear-coat finish

Delight the mother-to-be with this whimsical accessory.

Designed by Cynthia Moody Wheeler

❤ ❤ ❤ ❤ ❤ ❤ ❤ ❤ ❤ ❤ ❤ ❤ ❤ ❤ ❤ ❤ ❤

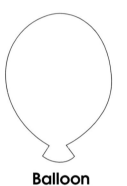

Balloon

Instructions

1. Trace 3 balloons onto paper side of Wonder-Under. Leaving approximate ½" margin, cut around Wonder-Under shapes. Press shapes onto wrong side of fabric scraps. Cut out shapes along pattern lines. Remove paper backing.

2. Position balloons onto light-switch plate. Fuse in place, one at a time. Using dimensional craft paint, outline balloons, adding freehand lines for balloon strings. Let dry.

3. Spray finished switch plate with several coats of clear-coat finish, letting dry between each coat.

Other Ideas

As the child grows older, make this accessory an annual gift by replacing the light-switch cover with one decorated with mature motifs.

Bear

Shirt

Starry Layette

Coordinate a crib set and rompers with your friend's nursery colors.
Stamp favorite phrases or messages with letters from the alphabet.

Designed by Dondra G. Parham

Materials
(for 1 baby item)

Fabric scraps (at least 5"
 square)
Romper, crib sheet, or
 blanket*
Pellon® Heavy Duty
 Wonder-Under®
Pinking shears
Cardboard wrapped in
 waxed paper
Textile medium
Acrylic craft paint
Small paintbrush
Alphabet stamps**

*For romper, cut 1 (2"
 square) and 1 small star.
 For sheet, cut 1 (3"
 square) and 1 medium
 star. For blanket, cut 1 (3"
 square) and 1 large star.
**Rubber stamps by Rubber
 Stampede®, available at
 stamping and craft stores.
 Or use alphabet patterns
 provided by tracing letters
 onto tracing paper and
 transferring them to baby
 item. Follow Step 4 to
 complete project.

Instructions

Note: For added security,
especially if items will be
washed frequently, outline
motifs with coordinating
dimensional fabric paint.

1. Wash, dry, and iron all
fabrics and baby item. Do
not use fabric softener in
washer or dryer.

2. Trace star pattern and
square onto paper side of
Wonder-Under. Leaving
approximate ½" margin, cut
around Wonder-Under
shapes. Press shapes onto
wrong side of fabrics. Cut
out shapes along pattern
lines. Trim edges of square
with pinking shears.
Remove paper backing.

3. Position square on baby
item as desired. Fuse in
place. Center and position
star on square. Fuse in
place.

4. Place covered cardboard
inside or underneath baby
item. Smooth area around
appliqué. Following manu-
facturer's instructions, mix
textile medium with craft
paint. Using paintbrush,
cover rubber stamp with
thin coat of paint. Stamp let-
ter on baby item around
appliqué. Repeat to finish
word or phrase. Let dry.

Other Ideas

Replace the stars and
squares with motifs cut
from novelty fabrics.

ABCDEFGHIJKLMNOPQRSTUVWXYZ

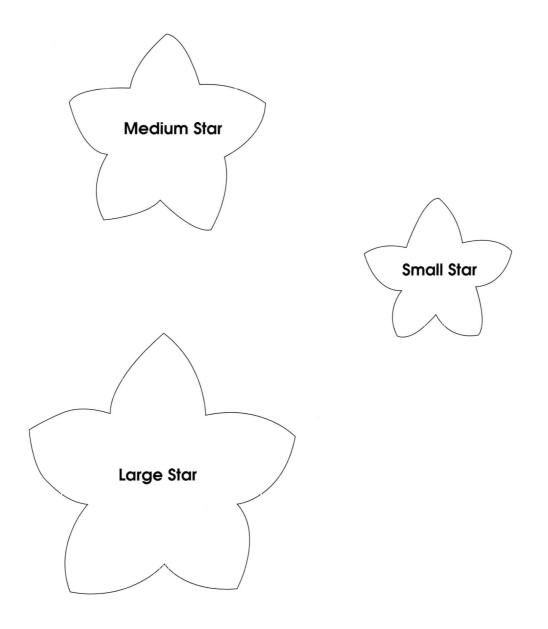

Medium Star

Small Star

Large Star

Child's Growth Chart

Materials

Pellon® Wonder-Under®
½ to 1 yard novelty fabric
  with large motifs
2 (60"-long) tape measures
Hot-glue gun and glue sticks
52" x 13" piece of felt
20"-long ¼"- to ½"-diameter
  dowel
24"-long piece of string
Permanent black fabric
  marker

Give new parents a clever way to track their child's growth through the years.

Designed by Heidi King

♥ ♥ ♥ ♥ ♥ ♥ ♥ ♥ ♥ ♥ ♥ ♥ ♥ ♥ ♥ ♥ ♥ ♥ ♥

Instructions

1. Press Wonder-Under onto wrong side of novelty fabric. Cut out enough desired motifs to decorate felt. Remove paper backing.

2. Cut both measuring tapes off at 12" mark. Referring to photo, hot-glue tapes on both edges of felt, aligning 12" ends with bottom edge.

3. Position and fuse motifs along length of felt. Cut 1 (2" x 13") strip of Wonder-Under. Press Wonder-Under onto wrong side of top edge of felt. Remove paper backing. Fold down top edge of felt at both 60" marks on measuring tapes. Fuse to back of felt, leaving space to insert dowel for hanging.

4. Insert dowel at top folded edge. Tie string to 1 end of dowel, 1" from dowel end. Repeat for other end.

5. Include a fabric marker with your gift for labeling chart.

Baby Blocks Lampshade

Materials

Pellon® Heavy Duty
  Wonder-Under®
Fabric scraps for appliqués
Dimensional fabric paint in
  squeeze bottle in color to
  coordinate with fabrics
Purchased plain fabric-
  covered lampshade

Fuse baby blocks to a lampshade for a lamp that's bound to be the focal point in a new nursery.

Designed by Cynthia Moody Wheeler

❤ ❤ ❤ ❤ ❤ ❤ ❤ ❤ ❤ ❤ ❤ ❤ ❤ ❤ ❤ ❤ ❤ ❤ ❤ ❤

Instructions

1. Trace 3 of each block pattern onto paper side of Wonder-Under. Leaving approximate ½" margin, cut around Wonder-Under shapes. Press shapes onto wrong side of fabrics. Cut out shapes along pattern lines. Remove paper backing.

2. Referring to photo, position blocks on lampshade. Fuse blocks in place one at a time.

3. Using dimensional fabric paint and following pattern lines, outline blocks with paint. Let dry.

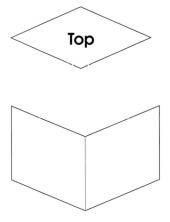

Top

Side

Gray line is painted line.

Christmas Gifts

Let us help you enjoy your holiday twice as much by offering you fresh gift ideas. With Pellon® Wonder-Under®, you can please a coworker with a merry coffee mug. Or get your kids involved this year by helping them make snowman pins for their teachers.

Present Perfect Tablecloth

Materials

Purchased tablecloth*
Fabric for appliqués: green, red**
Pellon® Heavy Duty Wonder-Under®
Fine-tip permanent black fabric marker

*We used a 54" square tablecloth.
**Yardage will depend on size of tablecloth used. We used ⅓ yard each of red and green for the tablecloth pictured.

It's easy to turn a plain white tablecloth into a stunning Christmas gift. Just cut package shapes from red and green fabrics, and fuse them to a purchased tablecloth.

Designed by Cynthia Moody Wheeler

★ ★ ★ ★ ★ ★ ★ ★ ★ ★ ★ ★ ★ ★ ★ ★ ★ ★ ★ ★

Instructions

Note: For added security, especially if tablecloth will be washed frequently, outline presents with coordinating dimensional fabric paint.

1. Wash, dry, and iron tablecloth and fabrics. Do not use fabric softener in washer or dryer.

2. To calculate number of presents needed, use the following formula: measure 1 side of tablecloth, subtract 20", divide by 7", round to nearest whole number, and multiply by 4.

3. For a 54" square tablecloth, trace 20 presents from page 124 onto paper side of Wonder-Under. (54" – 20" = 34"; 34" ÷ 7" = 4.8"; nearest whole number = 5; 5 x 4 = 20 presents.) Leaving approximate ½" margin, cut around Wonder-Under shapes. Press 10 Wonder-Under presents onto wrong side of red fabric. Press 10 Wonder-Under presents onto wrong side of green fabric. Cut out presents along pattern lines. Remove paper backing.

4. Referring to photo for placement, fuse presents on tablecloth along outer edges, alternating red and green presents.

5. Referring to pattern, use fabric marker to draw lines around knot and tails of bow.

Cut out shaded
areas.

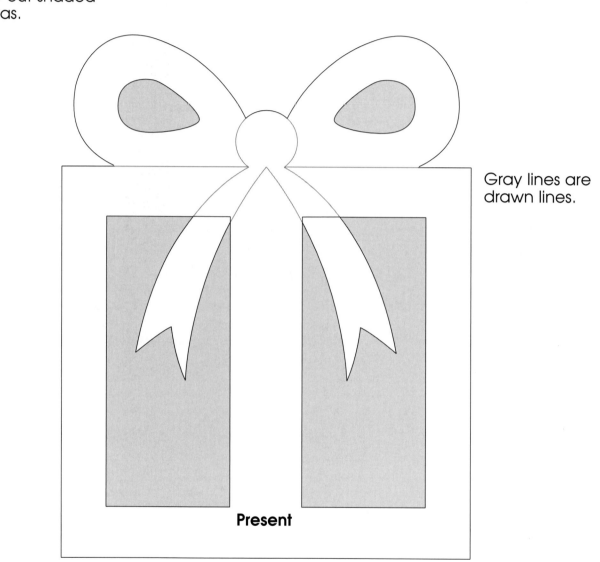

Gray lines are
drawn lines.

Present

Mitten Fun

Brighten up a friend's Christmas with an embellished vest.
Personalize the mitten appliqués with novelty fabrics, or decorate
solid-colored fabrics with fabric paint.

Designed by Heidi King

★ ★

Materials

Purchased plain denim vest
Pellon® Heavy Duty
    Wonder-Under®
Fabric for appliqués: ⅛ yard
    each red, green, navy
    acrylic felt
Gold dimensional fabric
    paint in squeeze bottle

Instructions

Note: Continue appliqués onto back of vest, if desired.

1. Wash, dry, and iron vest. Do not use fabric softener in washer or dryer. Trace 4 mittens and 3 mittens reversed onto paper side of Wonder-Under.

2. Leaving approximate ½" margin, cut around Wonder-Under shapes. Referring to photo for colors, press shapes onto felt. Cut out mittens along pattern lines. Remove paper backing. Fuse mittens onto vest.

3. Outline mittens with dimensional fabric paint. Add polka dots, squiggle lines, or zigzags. Referring to photo, finish mitten pairs with freehand lines.

Mitten
Trace. Reverse and trace again.

Christmas Spirit Apron

Make a festive apron for the holiday baker in your home. Kids will love gluing on the tiny tree ornaments. Novelty buttons and a purchased apron make this a quick and fun project.

Designed by Betsy Cooper Scott

★ ★

Materials

Purchased plain apron
Fabric for appliqués: ½ yard
   green, 4" square each red,
   yellow
Pellon® Heavy Duty
   Wonder-Under®
Assorted novelty shank but-
   tons (approximately 20)
Pliers
Washable fabric glue

Instructions

Note: For added security, especially if apron will be washed frequently, outline tree, star, and trunk with coordinating dimensional fabric paint.

1. Wash, dry, and iron apron and fabrics. Do not use fabric softener in washer or dryer. Trace 1 star, 1 trunk, and 1 tree (connect dots to complete pattern) onto paper side of Wonder-Under. Leaving approximate ½" margin, cut around Wonder-Under shapes. Referring to photo for colors, press shapes onto wrong side of fabrics. Cut out shapes along pattern lines. Remove paper backing.

2. Referring to photo, center and place trunk, tree, and star on front of apron. Fuse shapes in place.

3. Use pliers to snap off shanks from buttons. Arrange buttons on tree. Using fabric glue, glue each button in place. Let dry.

Star

Bottom of Tree

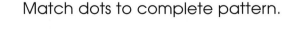

Match dots to complete pattern.

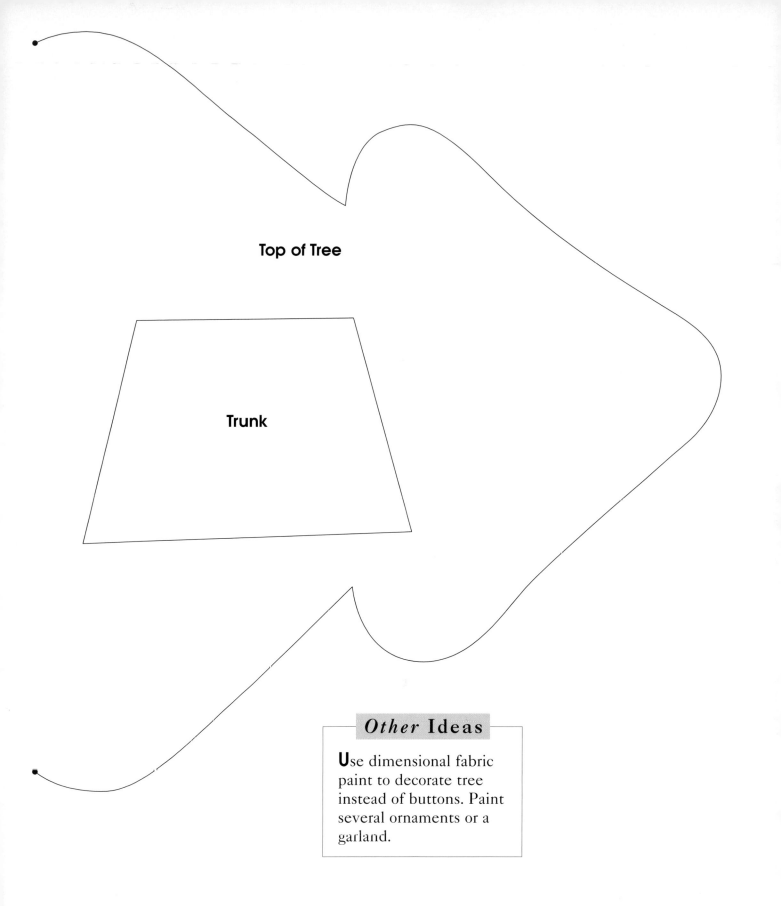

Top of Tree

Trunk

Match dots to complete pattern.

Candy-Coated Guest Towels

Fuse organdy-wrapped buttons to a set of purchased hand towels for a gift sweet enough for that special friend.

Designed by Dondra G. Parham

★ ★

Materials
(for 1 towel)

Linen guest towel
1 yard ⅛"-wide polka-dot
    ribbon
⅛ yard cotton organdy cut
    into 3 (4") squares
⅓ yard 1⅝"-wide plaid ribbon
¾"-wide Pellon® Wonder-
    Under® fusible tape
Narrow metal cake spatula
Pinking shears
Liquid ravel preventer
1⅛"-diameter covered button
    kit (3 buttons)
Pliers

Instructions

Note: Finished towel can be hand-washed in cold water. Lay flat to dry.

1. Wash, dry, and iron towel, ribbon, and fabric. Do not use fabric softener in washer or dryer. For button placement, measure and mark center of towel 2" from bottom edge. Measure and mark 2" on either side of center mark.

2. Cut 2 (3"-long) strips of Wonder-Under tape. Cut each strip in half lengthwise (Diagram A). Set 1 strip aside. Press 1 strip of Wonder-Under to edge of 1 organdy square (Diagram B). Remove paper backing. Roll organdy square to form a tube until edge overlaps Wonder-Under strip (Diagram C). Slide spatula into tube to form pressing surface for fusing edges together. Press overlapping edges to Wonder-Under strip. Use pinking shears to trim open ends of tube. Apply liquid ravel preventer to pinked edges. Let dry. Repeat to make 2 more tubes.

3. Cut plaid ribbon into 3"-long pieces. Following manufacturer's instructions on button kit, cover 3 buttons with ribbon. Use pliers to snap off button shanks.

4. Cut polka-dot ribbon into 6 equal lengths. Slide 1 button into 1 tube, positioning fused seam at back of button. Center button and twist ends of tube to resemble wrapped candy. Tie and knot each end with polka-dot ribbon. Apply 1 drop of liquid ravel preventer to each knot. Let dry. Trim ribbon ends at equal lengths. Apply liquid ravel preventer to ends. Repeat to make 2 more wrapped candies.

5. Cut 3 (1"-long) pieces of Wonder-Under tape. Center pieces over button marks on towel. Press Wonder-Under pieces onto towel. Remove paper backing from 1 Wonder-Under piece. Center 1 wrapped candy on Wonder-Under piece. Flip candy and towel over. Fuse candy in place, using button back as pressing surface. Repeat for remaining candies.

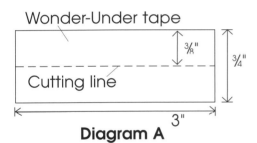

Diagram A

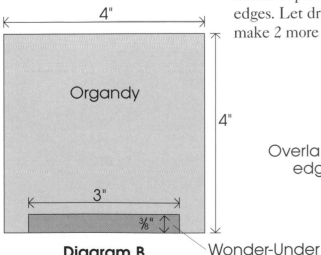

Diagram B

Wonder-Under

Diagram C

Santa Stocking

Materials

Purchased stocking with contrasting cuff*

Fabric scraps for appliqués: ¼ yard green; ⅛ yard each cranberry red, white-on-white; 6" square each black, red print, Christmas print, green print, gold print

Pellon® Heavy Duty Wonder-Under®

Red colored pencil (optional)

Dimensional fabric paints in squeeze bottles: green, cranberry red, silver, black, gold

* Stocking (1118) by Bag-Works. See page 160 for more information.

Welcome Santa and his elves with this no-sew appliqué stocking. Stuffed or empty, it makes a splendid gift.

Designed by Michele Crawford

★ ★ ★ ★ ★ ★ ★ ★ ★ ★ ★ ★ ★ ★ ★ ★ ★ ★ ★ ★

Instructions

1. Wash, dry, and iron stocking and fabrics. Do not use fabric softener in washer or dryer.

2. Using patterns below and on pages 140–141, trace onto paper side of Wonder-Under 1 large star, 1 small star, 1 rectangular package, 2 square packages, 1 hat, 1 coat, 1 belt, 1 boot, 1 boot reversed, 2 mittens, 1 tree, 1 face, 2 cuff furs, 2 hat furs, and 2 coat furs. Leaving approximate ½" margin, cut out Wonder-Under shapes. Referring to photo for colors, press shapes onto wrong side of fabrics. Cut out shapes along pattern lines.

3. Remove paper backing from 1 cuff fur, 1 hat fur, and 1 coat fur. Fuse each piece onto its duplicate.

4. Referring to photo, arrange pieces on stocking front. Fuse pieces in layers, beginning with tree.

5. Color cheeks on face with colored pencil, if desired. Outline appliqués with coordinating dimensional fabric paint. Using paint, draw ribbon bows on packages, laces on boots, buckle on belt, and eyes and nose on face. Let dry after each application.

Large Star

13

Square Package

12

Rectangular Package

11

Small Star

14

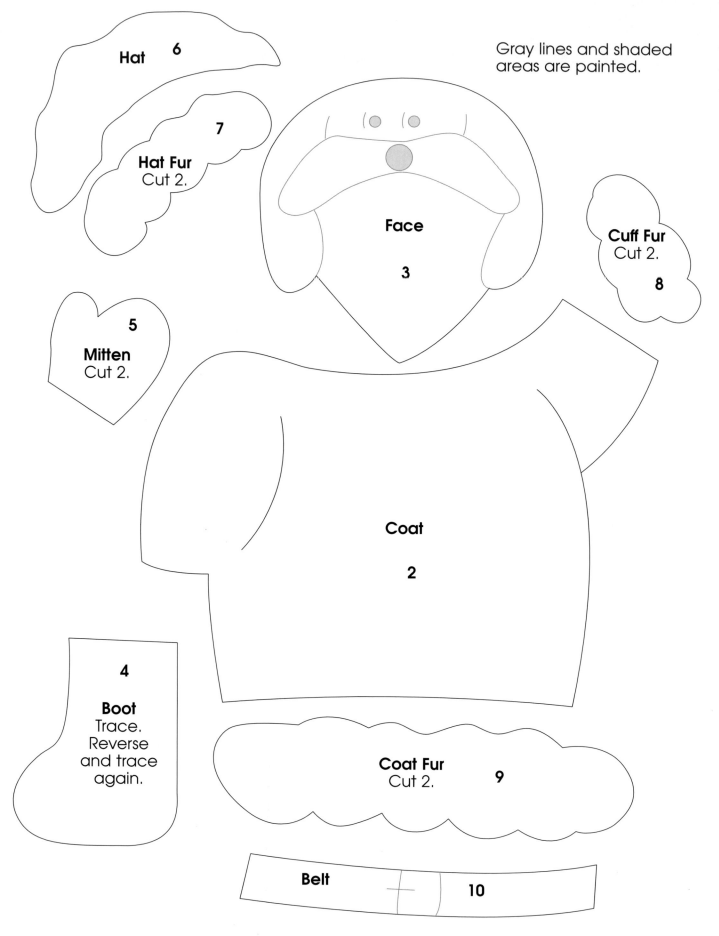

Hat 6

Hat Fur
Cut 2. 7

Gray lines and shaded
areas are painted.

Face

3

Cuff Fur
Cut 2.

8

5

Mitten
Cut 2.

Coat

2

4

Boot
Trace.
Reverse
and trace
again.

Coat Fur
Cut 2. 9

Belt 10

Tree

1

Especially-for-You Christmas Cards

Send holiday greetings to someone special with a handmade Christmas card. Using fabric scraps and Pellon® Wonder-Under®, it's easy to embellish plain cards and matching envelopes.

Designed by Carol A. Burger

★ ★

Materials

For each:
Pellon® Wonder-Under®
Fabric scraps for appliqués
Purchased blank card and
  envelope
Fine-tip permanent black
  marker

For Angel Card:
Powdered blush and brush
  (optional)

For Snowman Card:
White felt square
⅜"-wide (4-hole) button
Hot-glue gun and glue sticks

Instructions for Watering Can Card

Note: Use a dry iron to fuse fabric to paper. Dry heat keeps the paper smooth.

1. Trace 1 watering can, 1 of each ribbon, 1 (⅜"-diameter) circle (cut in half for 2 ladybugs), 14 (¼"-diameter) circles for holly berries, and 12 holly leaves onto paper side of Wonder-Under. Leaving approximate ½" margin, cut around Wonder-Under shapes. Referring to photo for colors, press shapes onto wrong side of fabrics. Cut out shapes along pattern lines. Remove paper backing.

2. Referring to photo, position and center watering can, ribbons, holly leaves, and holly berries, in that order, on front of card. Entwine holly leaves and ribbons as desired. Place 1 ladybug on end of ribbon. Fuse pieces in place.

3. Using black marker, draw dashed lines around holly leaf edges to resemble sewn stitches. Draw dashed lines in center of holly leaves. Draw round head and antennae on ladybug body.

4. For envelope, fuse holly leaves, berries, and remaining ladybug to bottom corner of envelope front. Follow Step 3 to finish.

Instructions for Angel Card

1. Trace 5 stars and 1 angel (pieces 1–7) onto paper side of Wonder-Under. Leaving approximate ½" margin, cut around Wonder-Under shapes. Referring to photo for colors, press shapes onto wrong side of fabrics. Cut out shapes along pattern lines. Remove paper backing.

2. Referring to photo, position and center angel pieces 1–7, in that order, on front of card. Fuse pieces in place.

Holly Leaf

Ribbons

Star

Angel

1   5   1

2   2

4

6

7

3   3

Gray lines are drawn lines.

Dashes indicate lines of underlying pattern pieces.

Watering Can

3. Using black marker, draw dashed lines around stars, angel wings, head, arms, hands, legs, and dress pocket to resemble sewn stitches. Add eyes, halo, and hair as desired. Referring to photo, draw a line from angel hand to star. Using blush, brush circles of color on angel face, if desired.

4. For envelope, fuse 2 stars to bottom corner of envelope front. Using black marker, draw dashed lines around stars as in Step 3. Referring to photo, draw a line from star to star, connecting top points.

Instructions for Snowman Card

1. Trace 1 snowman (pieces 1–10), 1 bird (piece 11), 1 bird reversed, 1 bird's scarf (piece 12), 1 bird's scarf reversed, 1 birdhouse (pieces 1–5), and 1 holly leaf from page 145 onto paper side of Wonder-Under. Leaving approximate ½" margin, cut around Wonder-Under shapes. Referring to photo for colors, fuse shapes onto wrong side of fabrics. Press Wonder-Under pieces 8 and 9 onto felt. Cut out shapes along pattern lines. Remove paper backing.

2. Referring to photo, position the following pieces on card: birdhouse pieces 1–5, snowman pieces 1–10, and bird pieces 11–12, in that order. Fuse shapes in place.

3. Referring to photo and using black marker, draw dashed lines around snowman, snowman hat, snowman scarf, bird's scarf, and birdhouse snow edges to resemble sewn stitches. Add eyes and mouth. Add fringe to snowman and bird's scarf.

4. Hot-glue button onto birdhouse.

5. For envelope, fuse bird, scarf, and holly leaf onto bottom corner of envelope front. Using black marker, draw dashed lines around pieces as in Step 3. Draw line in center of holly leaf.

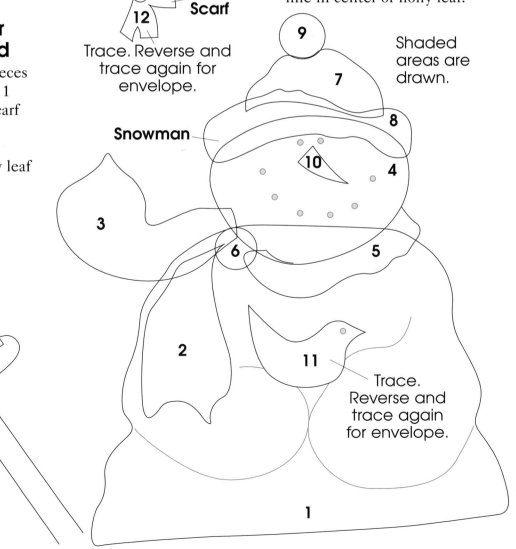

Bird's Scarf

Trace. Reverse and trace again for envelope.

Snowman

Shaded areas are drawn.

Trace. Reverse and trace again for envelope.

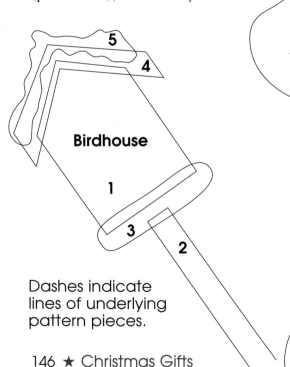

Birdhouse

Dashes indicate lines of underlying pattern pieces.

Under-Wraps Pillow Cover

Make holiday decorating easier on your friends by giving them Christmas pillow wraps for their homes. Coordinate napkin choices and motifs with their decor.

Designed by Cynthia Moody Wheeler

Materials
(for 1 pillow cover)

2 purchased 18" square cloth
napkins with plain
centers*
Fabric scraps for appliqués:
4" square each cream
Ultrasuede®, light peach,
brown print
Pellon® Heavy Duty
Wonder-Under®
Gold glitter dimensional fabric paint in squeeze bottle
Paintbrush
1 yard (⅜"-wide) satin ribbon
to coordinate with napkin
Purchased plain pillow
4 small rubber bands

*The napkin pictured is
from Williams-Sonoma.

Instructions

1. Wash, dry, and iron napkins, fabric, and ribbon.
Trace 1 manger, 1 baby face,
and 1 baby blanket onto
paper side of Wonder-Under.
Leaving approximate ½"
margin, cut around Wonder-
Under shapes. Referring to
photo for colors, press
Wonder-Under shapes onto
wrong side of fabrics. Cut out
pieces along pattern lines.
Remove paper backing.

2. Center and position baby
face, baby blanket, and
manger, in that order, on
1 napkin. Fuse each piece
onto napkin.

3. Using pattern as guide,
gold paint, and paintbrush,
paint halo around baby's
face and head. Let dry.
(Note: Paint will be cloudy
when wet, but will dry gold.)
Referring to pattern and
using same paint, add star to
upper right-hand corner of
napkin center. Let dry.

4. Cut ribbon into 4 equal
lengths. Position napkins on
pillow diagonally, 1 on front
of pillow and 1 on back,
matching corners. "Tie"
each corner with a rubber
band. Tie ribbon bows over
rubber bands.

Other Ideas

Decorate your home with pillow wraps year-
round. Make wraps inspired by your favorite
holiday, such as Easter, Halloween, or
Thanksgiving.

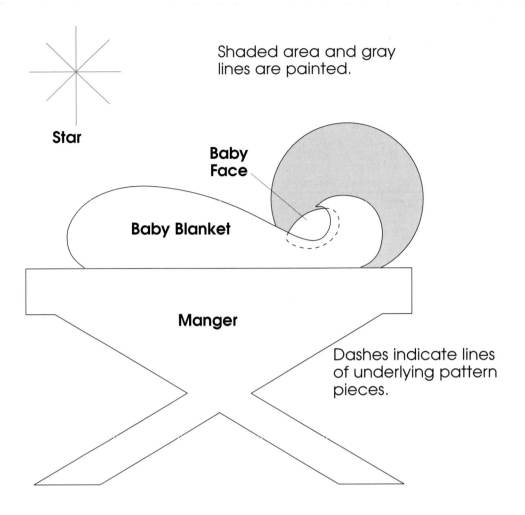

Shaded area and gray
lines are painted.

Star

**Baby
Face**

Baby Blanket

Manger

Dashes indicate lines
of underlying pattern
pieces.

Jolly Felt Pins

Your kids can join in the fun and help make these holiday pins for family, friends, and neighbors.

Designed by Carol A. Burger

★ ★

Materials
(for 1 pin)

For both:
Pellon® Heavy Duty Wonder-Under®
Red fabric scraps for appliqués
White felt square
⅛ yard canvas
Fine-tip permanent black fabric marker
Powdered blush and brush (optional)
White embroidery floss
Hot-glue gun and glue sticks
½"-diameter (4-hole) button
Pin fastener

For Santa:
Light peach fabric scrap for appliqué

For Snowman:
Green fabric scrap for appliqué
3 (5-mm) half-round black beads
Felt-tip permanent red marker
Toothpick

Instructions for Santa

1. Trace 1 Santa hat, 1 Santa hat brim, 1 Santa face, and 1 Santa beard, onto paper side of Wonder-Under. Leaving approximate ½" margin, cut around Wonder-Under shapes. Referring to photo for colors, press Wonder-Under shapes onto wrong side of fabrics. For beard and hat brim, press Wonder-Under onto felt. For Santa face, press Wonder-Under onto wrong side of light peach fabric. Cut out pieces along pattern lines. Remove paper backing.

2. Using square of canvas for base, position hat, face, hat brim, and beard, in that order, on canvas. Remove beard. Draw eyes with marker. Using blush, add color to face, if desired. Fuse each piece to canvas, ending with beard. Trim canvas close to edges.

3. Loop embroidery floss 4 or 5 times into 2¼"-long loops. Tie and knot center of loop bundle with short piece of floss. Hot-glue bundle, knot side down, onto center top of Santa beard.

4. Referring to photo, tie and knot floss through holes of button. Trim ends. Hot-glue button onto Santa hat brim. Hot-glue pin fastener onto back of Santa.

Instructions for Snowman

1. Trace 1 snowman, 1 snowman hatband, 1 snowman hat, 1 scarf, and 1 scarf reversed onto paper side of Wonder-Under. Leaving ½" margin, cut around Wonder-Under shapes. Referring to photo for colors, press Wonder-Under shapes onto wrong side of fabrics. For snowman, press Wonder-Under onto felt. Cut out pieces along pattern lines. Remove paper backing.

2. Fuse 2 scarves together with Wonder-Under in the middle.

3. Using square of canvas for base, position the following pieces on canvas: snowman, hat, and hatband, in that order. Fuse each piece to canvas one at a time. Trim canvas close to edges.

4. Draw eyes with black marker. Use blush to add color to cheeks, if desired.

5. Hot-glue scarf onto snowman neck. Referring to photo, tie and knot piece of floss through holes of button. Trim ends. Hot-glue button onto scarf. Hot-glue 3 black beads onto front.

6. Using red marker, color one-half of toothpick. Snap toothpick off ½" below red point. Pierce broken end of toothpick through felt until ¹⁄₁₆" is showing through back of snowman. Hot-glue pin fastener over toothpick end on back of snowman.

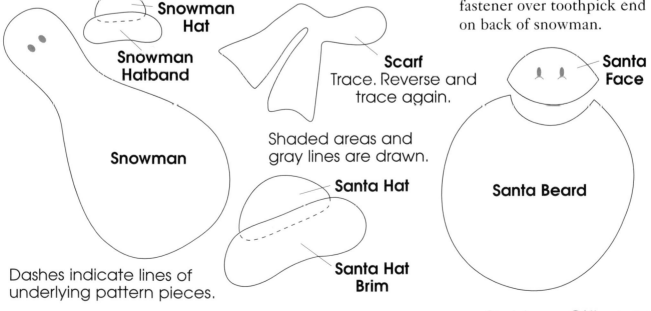

Snowman Hat

Snowman Hatband

Snowman

Scarf
Trace. Reverse and trace again.

Shaded areas and gray lines are drawn.

Santa Hat

Santa Hat Brim

Santa Face

Santa Beard

Dashes indicate lines of underlying pattern pieces.

Ornamental Sweatshirt

Materials

Purchased plain sweatshirt
Fabric for appliqués: 6"
    square each red, gold,
    green
Pellon® Wonder-Under®
Gold glitter dimensional fabric paint in squeeze bottle

Warm up someone's holiday evening with this sparkly sweatshirt. Fused shapes, finished with dimensional glitter paint make for a sensational, but easy gift.

Designed by Cynthia Moody Wheeler

★ ★

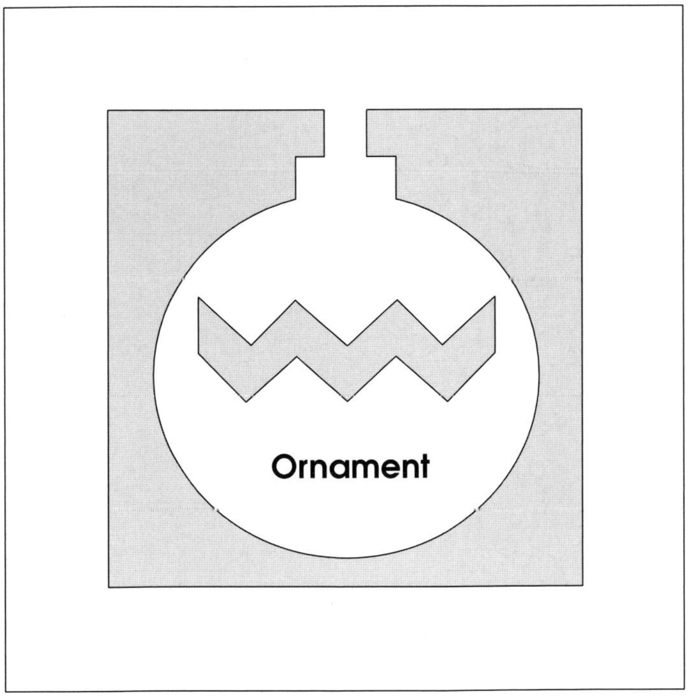

Instructions

1. Wash, dry, and iron sweatshirt and fabrics. Do not use fabric softener in washer or dryer.

2. Trace 3 ornaments onto paper side of Wonder-Under. Leaving approximate ½" margin, cut around Wonder-Under shapes. Press 1 shape onto wrong side of each fabric square. Cut out ornaments along pattern lines. Cut out shaded areas. Remove paper backing.

3. Referring to photo, center and position ornaments on front of sweatshirt. Fuse ornaments to sweatshirt.

4. Outline each ornament with dimensional fabric paint. Let dry. *(Note:* Paint will be cloudy when wet, but will dry gold.)

Ornament

Cut out shaded areas.

Angelic Place Setting

Materials
(for 1 napkin and 1 place mat)

For both:
¼ yard yellow fabric
Pellon® Heavy Duty
  Wonder-Under®
Fine-tip permanent black
  fabric marker

For Napkin:
Purchased plain napkin

For Place Mat:
Purchased plain place mat
Fabric for appliqués: ¼ yard
  each green, burgundy;
  ⅛ yard pale peach
Powdered blush and brush
  (optional)

Bring an angel to dinner when you give this place mat and napkin set to your host. Use novelty fabrics and your friend's favorite colors to make your angel magical.

Designed by Carol A. Burger

★ ★ ★ ★ ★ ★ ★ ★ ★ ★ ★ ★ ★ ★ ★ ★ ★ ★ ★ ★

Instructions for Napkin

1. Wash, dry, and iron napkin and fabrics. Do not use fabric softener in washer or dryer.

2. Trace 1 small star and 2 medium stars onto paper side of Wonder-Under. Leaving approximate ½" margin, cut around shapes. Press shapes onto yellow fabric. Cut out stars along pattern lines. Remove paper backing.

3. Referring to photo, position stars on bottom edge of napkin as desired. Fuse each star in place.

4. Using fabric marker, draw dashed lines around each star to resemble sewn stitches.

Instructions for Place Mat

1. Wash, dry, and iron place mat and fabrics. Do not use fabric softener in washer or dryer.

2. Using patterns below and on pages 156–157, trace onto paper side of Wonder-Under 1 small star, 2 medium stars,

Small Star

Large Star

Medium Star

2 large stars, 2 wings, 2 hands, 2 arms, and 1 each of patterns 3–7. Leaving approximate ½" margin, cut out shapes.

3. Referring to photo, press shapes onto wrong side of fabrics. *Note:* Press Wonder-Under pattern piece 4 onto right side of coordinating fabric. Cut out shapes along pattern lines. Remove paper backing.

4. Following pattern lines and numbers, arrange shapes on center of place mat, starting with piece 1 and ending with piece 7. Fuse shapes in place. Referring to photo, position stars around angel as desired. Fuse each star in place.

5. Using fabric marker, draw eyes. Draw dashed lines around each star, angel head, hands, legs, and dress, to resemble sewn stitches. If desired, add blush to angel cheeks and knees.

Wing
Trace. Reverse
and trace again.

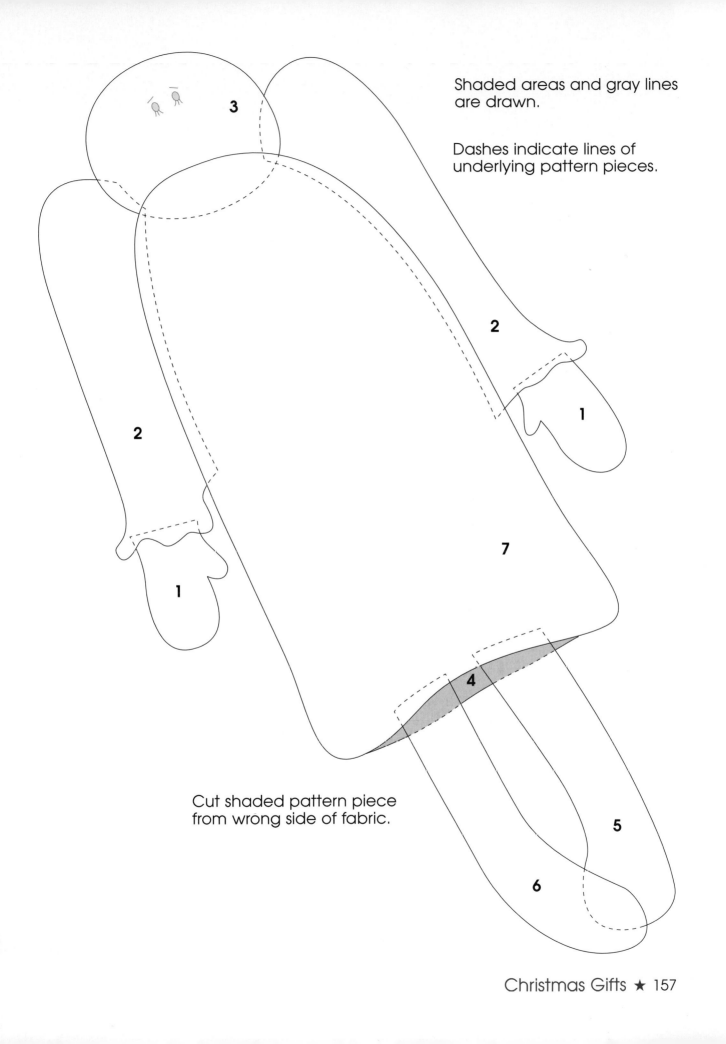

Shaded areas and gray lines
are drawn.

Dashes indicate lines of
underlying pattern pieces.

Cut shaded pattern piece
from wrong side of fabric.

Stacked-Ribbon Tree Ornaments

Materials
(for 1 ornament)

Pellon® Heavy Duty
    Wonder-Under®
Dark green felt square
    (1 (8½" x 11") felt square
    makes 6 ornaments)
1 yard (⅝"-wide) green
    grosgrain ribbon
4"-long gold cord or gold
    metallic thread
Pinking shears
1 cinnamon stick
Liquid ravel preventer
Hot-glue gun and glue sticks

What better way to involve your kids in Christmas giving than with these easy tree ornaments? One or two are just right to give teachers and friends. They even have the sweet smell of cinnamon.

Designed by Barbara McNorton Neel

★ ★

Instructions

1. Trace 1 tree onto paper side of Wonder-Under. Leaving approximate ½" margin, cut around tree. Press Wonder-Under tree onto felt. Cut out tree along pattern lines. Remove paper backing.

2. Working from Wonder-Under side, align ribbon along bottom edge of felt tree. Fuse ribbon to tree. Trim ribbon. Repeat for following rows of ribbon, until felt is covered.

3. Before fusing last row of ribbon, loop gold cord to form hanger. Center ends of loop at top of tree and fuse ribbon, sandwiching hanger between felt and ribbon.

4. Using pinking shears, trim sides of tree only, leaving bottom untrimmed. Apply liquid ravel preventer to cut sides of tree.

5. Center and hot-glue cinnamon stick vertically to back of tree at lower edge.

Tree

Acknowledgments

SPECIAL THANKS...

...to the following people and companies for their valuable contributions toward project development:

Carol E. Burger

Michele Crawford

Phyllis Dunstan

Alisa Jane Hyde

Heidi T. King

Françoise Dudal Kirkman

Barbara McNorton Neel

Dondra G. Parham

Susan G. Peele

Betsy Cooper Scott

Carol Tipton

Cynthia Moody Wheeler

Lois Winston

Nancy Worrell

We especially want to thank the talented staffs at **Leisure Arts Inc.** and **Freudenberg Nonwovens**, and in particular **Anne Van Wagner Childs, Gloria Bearden,** and **Jane Schenck.**

ORDERING INFORMATION

To locate a Pellon® Wonder-Under® retailer in your area, call 1-800-223-5275.

For more information on canvas items, contact: BagWorks, 3301 C South Cravens Road, Ft. Worth, TX 76119; (817) 446-8080. Check their web site at http://www.bagworks.com or send $2 for a catalog.